The Angel Oracle

The Angel Oracle

How to bring angelic help into your life

Wendy Hobson

ARCTURUS

I would like to extend my thanks to everyone who shared the accounts of their angelic encounters with me, and to Lauren (http://www.ainglkiss.com/angels/), who introduced me to some of those who had experienced such an encounter.

The information in this book is provided for guidance only and does not constitute the practice of medicine. Readers are specifically advised to consult their GP or other medical professional about any issue related to physical or mental well-being. In particular, some essential oils are contra-indicated in pregnancy or if you have certain chronic conditions.

ARCTURUS

This edition published in 2012 by Arcturus Publishing Limited
26/27 Bickels Yard, 151–153 Bermondsey Street,
London SE1 3HA

ISBN: 978-1-84837-998-5
AD002006EN

Printed in Singapore

Contents

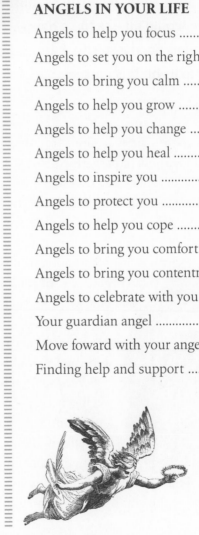

Get in touch with your angel oracle

Every life has its positives and negatives, but whatever our circumstances we would all like to be happy. To achieve happiness, most of us need a spiritual dimension. Looking to the angels can help us on this journey.

Perhaps you believe in the Christian God, or in the divine in another form. It may be that you believe only in a spiritual dimension, or perhaps you are sceptical about the whole spiritual discussion. Believer or unbeliever, devout or sceptic, there is food for thought in these pages.

Whether you believe this life is an end in itself, or a stepping-stone to a better one makes no difference to the logic of the assumption that we should all strive to make it the best life we can.

For each of us, this means something completely different. We cannot choose our parents or our circumstances; we all come into the world helpless and at the mercy of our genes and our environment. But at some point we have to take responsibility for ourselves and how we choose to live. For most of us, reaching that maturity is a gradual process, but by the time we are verging on adulthood we should at least be beginning to find our own path, taking control of our place in the world and assuming responsibility for our actions.

> '**Most folks are about as happy as they make up their minds to be.**'
> Abraham Lincoln (1809–1865),
> US President

For those born with any combination of sound health, good looks, intelligence, talents, a stable, secure environment and, above all, a loving family, achieving this objective may not be too hard. At the other end of the spectrum, for those living in difficult circumstances, the challenges are immense. Most of us fall between the two extremes, but for all of us the goal is the same. Whether you have a mountain to climb or just a gentle slope, whether you call it contentment, peace or

spiritual enlightenment, the main thing most of us want is to be happy.

There is no single definition of happiness because it means something different to each of us, and even people who claim to be happy may not be able to tell you why. So it stands to reason that if happiness is to be found at so many destinations, there have to be myriad routes to get there.

This book is about one such route, although we may find the road has many branches. It is about finding a spiritual dimension – perhaps religious, perhaps not, perhaps internal, perhaps external – that you can reach out to, and that can support you, protect you and guide you towards whatever goals you set yourself.

So who are these spiritual guides? They may be messengers from the divine, or sources of light or energy, or beings we can call upon, or a state of mind to which we aspire. Whatever form they take, these guides can bring us light, love and even enlightenment.

We will call them angels.

The revelations of the angel oracle

In this book we will try to show you how to tune in to your own inner angel. So why is it called *The Angel Oracle*? Is it about revelation and prophecy, which are the core of the dictionary definition of the word 'oracle'? Yes it is, but perhaps not in the way you might think. The oracles we read about in the ancient world were mystics, usually women, visited at times of trauma or called upon to guide the footsteps of someone having to make a difficult – sometimes impossible – choice. Usually weird, almost certainly high on something, and reliably confusing, the common factor always seems to be that they put the onus of the decision on the person seeking help. They didn't solve anyone's problems; what they did so effectively was to act as a catalyst that prompted the subjects to find a solution for themselves.

For that is the key: no one can tell you how to live your life, how to make decisions or how to find comfort or love. It's really up to you.

That is a hard truth to come to terms with, but also a liberating one. When we cease to look for excuses for our behaviour and its consequences, or someone to solve our issues for us, then we are more likely to roll up our sleeves and deal with what life throws at us. As the saying goes, 'if you find yourself hock deep in horse manure, you'd better learn to shovel'. It is brutal but sound advice!

While we may be able to fend for ourselves, it doesn't mean we don't need the support and help of those around us. If we are lucky, we may have a network of friends and family on whom we can rely. The support of others can afford us security and peace of mind, but it doesn't take away our responsibility.

Have you been in the situation of knowing the right thing for someone else to do, but believing they must find the answer for themselves? If you have children, you will have experienced the frustration of knowing that the toy will break and there will be tears before bedtime if he keeps dropping it from the top of the climbing frame, or that this particular friend will always be late, or that the boyfriend will let her down.

In those situations, how do you help your children? You can tell them what the consequences of their actions are likely to be. You can show them by example. You can set up protective mechanisms to mitigate the problem or deflect any danger. If none of those things works, you can be there to support, comfort or commiserate when things go wrong or, indeed, celebrate when they turn out right. Between parent and child, between family members and friends, there is a web of mutual support and affection.

That web could be said to be a mirror of our relationship with angels. On a spiritual level, they can be our guide, protector or comforter. They cannot always solve our problems but they can help us to reveal ourselves and to find our own solutions. They can act as the catalyst we need in order to reveal the truth of the situation we are in and show us how to discover the best thing to do.

Our inner oracle

To be able to reach that angelic advice, we need to learn the appropriate techniques, practise them and, above all, allow ourselves to be open to the guidance we receive.

We all possess, deep inside our psyche, an indefinable element that knows what is best for us, and what is the right thing to do in the circumstances in which we find ourselves. It is partly our moral code, which we have all seen illustrated in films as the angel on one shoulder and the devil on the other, each one pushing his own point of view. But it is more than that, because it is subjective; it holds us at the centre of our decision-making. We can call that our inner oracle, and it is through that oracle that we can make contact with the angels.

Through various techniques, which we will look at

'Health is the greatest gift, contentment the greatest wealth, faithfulness the best relationship.'
Buddha (563–483BC), Hindu Prince Gautama Siddharta, founder of Buddhism

in turn, we will show you how to initiate that contact. You are unlikely to see a winged being, the traditional image we associate with angels. The journey may take you to a spiritual dimension in which you experience angelic contact: a real, apparently physical contact with a spiritual being. It may take you deep inside yourself and give you a real understanding of your inner angel oracle. Either way, this spiritual intuition – this angel oracle – is something we would all benefit from learning to listen to and understand.

The Angelic Realms

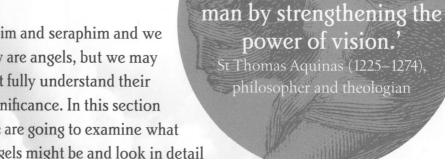

'An angel can illuminate the thought and mind of man by strengthening the power of vision.'
St Thomas Aquinas (1225–1274), philosopher and theologian

We have all heard of cherubim and seraphim and we are probably aware that they are angels, but we may not fully understand their significance. In this section we are going to examine what angels might be and look in detail at some angels whose names and characteristics have been defined.

As part of the exercise of defining the angels we are going to be working with, we will also delve into our inner angel oracle to try to understand what kind of guidance it can give us.

According to the Oxford English Dictionary, an angel is an attendant or messenger of God, usually represented in human form with wings. A secondary and more mundane definition is of a very virtuous and caring person; these are the qualities we generally associate with angels.

> 'For thou hast made him a little lower than the angels.'
>
> Psalms 8 : 5

The religious context

The concept of angels is very much part of the Judaeo-Christian tradition and it is with this religion that they are most commonly associated. Created by God before he created humans, they are beings of a higher order than us, residing with God in his heaven and filling the plane above us.

Although mentioned frequently in the Bible, they are only occasionally named and so, like the 'three wise men' of the Nativity, a web of information has been spun around them. We know from the Bible that they are spiritual beings of pure goodness, standing before God and constantly praising him. Structured into a hierarchy of three choirs – which also have various definitions – the seraphim, cherubim and thrones are nearest to God, followed by the dominions, virtues and powers, and finally by the principalities, the archangels and the angels.

The primary function of the third choir of angels is to act as a liaison, or a means of communication, between humans and God both to protect humans and to open up their spiritual potential. As each angel has particular qualities or virtues, they focus on helping humankind in the most appropriate ways.

In addition, some sources claim that everyone possesses a guardian angel, who looks after and protects his protégé throughout life.

The cultural context

It is far from true, however, that the idea of angels is solely part of the Christian tradition since similar beings exist in earlier cultures. The word 'cherabim' is derived from *karabu*, the name of the protective gods of the Ancient Assyrians. The Ancient Greek *daimones* provided a similar link between humans and the gods, while the Ancient Roman *genii* – one good, the other evil – provide the inspiration for our guardian angels.

The idea of a benevolent spirit, separate from us and above us, possibly with a higher spiritual power, is common in many cultures. Such spirits are usually protective of our spiritual and physical needs, guarding us from ourselves and sometimes from the malevolent influence of other spiritual beings.

Angels appear in other traditions too; for example, in spiritualism, where the living commune with the spirits of the dead. Many cultures believe that these are the spirits of people who have died, but have elevated their spiritual awareness to such a point that they have risen to a higher plane. Spiritualists

believe that people become angels when they die, which is a comforting
thought when you have lost a loved one, but is not something that is
documented in the traditional scriptures.

In Native-American tradition, such spirits of the dead often manifest
as animals and can imbue any human with whom they associate with the
powers of that animal. This explains the chosen names of some famous
Native Americans, such as Bald Eagle or Running Bear.

Angels, however, are almost always represented in human form, usually
tall and beautiful and frequently androgynous. Often sporting a halo, they are
generally pictured with huge, splendid wings.

The psychological context

For those without a religious commitment, angels or superior spirits still have an important role to play.
They can represent a spiritual energy or a concept of goodness to which we can aspire or attempt to find
in ourselves – our inner angel oracle, that spiritual element that helps and guides us through our lives if
only we are open to its advice. Even those who are not 'believers' can usually conceive of a dimension or
of occurrences that defy logic. Sometimes we just have to take things on faith.

What are angels?

The first challenge here is the question: 'What are angels?'. There are many definitions, but some elements are constant, so we will begin by looking at the features most people associate with angels.

Angelic characteristics

Angels are found across many religions and cultures. There is much cross-fertilization of ideas and many of their characteristics are recognizable even in different traditions. In the same way that early Christians superimposed their beliefs and traditions onto existing pagan celebrations – for example, we celebrate the Christian festival of Easter at the same time as Eostre, the pagan festival of spring – many angelic characteristics mix and match elements from different religions, cultures and parts of the world.

The Bible is the source of much of our information about angels and, for Christians, it is the only accurate source. As servants of a benevolent God, angels are obviously beings of spirit, existing on a higher plane than mortals. They exist in another dimension and are always associated with light and the force of positive energy. They are mentioned many times in the Bible as being in God's presence and able to look on His face, so they are always holy, pure and supremely good.

> '...for I tell you that in heaven, their angels always behold the face of my Father who is in heaven.'
>
> Matthew 18 : 10

'It is not known precisely where angels dwell — whether in the air, the void, or the planets. It has not been God's pleasure that we should be informed of their abode.'

Voltaire (1694–1778), writer and philosopher

Our word 'angel' is derived from the Ancient Greek *angelos*, meaning 'messenger'; the Hebrew and Persian names *malakh* and *angaros* also define angels as messengers of God. Clearly one of the outstanding examples for Christians is the message that Gabriel brought to the young and innocent Mary, that she would bear a child who would be the son of God.

'And, behold, thou
shalt conceive in thy
womb, and bring
forth a son, and shall
call his name Jesus.'

Luke 1 : 31

This is just one example. Throughout the Bible there are many accounts of angels acting as messengers: from angels appearing to Noah to tell him to build the ark, to angels appearing to Jacob in his dreams. In this role, they often act as intermediaries between God and mankind, a channel of communication reminding us of God's goodness and, sometimes, of human waywardness, perhaps warning the righteous to escape God's anger at human wickedness.

But even when they are chastizing, angels have our best interests at heart and are responsive to human need. They are there to help and protect us when we are in trouble.

> **'And behold, the angel of the Lord came upon him, and a light shined in the prison: and he smote Peter on the side, and raised him up, saying, Arise up quickly. And his chains fell from his hands.'**
>
> ACTS 12 : 7

In the example above, as in many other instances, the disciple Peter experiences the angelic encounter as though in a dream or a vision, only realizing after the event that he was delivered from Herod's prison by an angel.

In some Christian contexts, there is the idea that people can become like the angels after they die, raising the possibility that we all have the potential to become angels. This fits with the idea in some descriptions that angels are innumerable, although other sources suggest that the number of angels is finite.

The Bible does not actually state that we have the potential to become angels. Spiritualists believe we can contact the spirits of people who have passed away and sometimes refer to them as angels.

In the Islamic religion, angels figure strongly. Allah is surrounded by billions of angels, which he created from light. One of the most prominent Christian angels, Gabriel, is also the angel who appeared to Mohammad to tell him about his role as a prophet and to teach him about religion. As an essential part

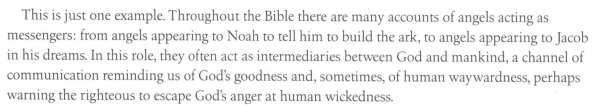

'and when the morning arose, then the angels hastened Lot, saying, Arise, take thy wife, and thy two daughters, which are here; lest thou be consumed in the iniquity of the city.'

Genesis 19 :15

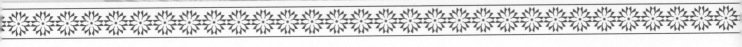

of daily life, angels are thought by many to represent the conscience, as each of us is accompanied throughout our life by two angels, one on each shoulder. The angel on the right shoulder records all our good deeds; the angel on the left takes account of the less noble ones. On the Day of Judgement, each individual will have to account for everything recorded by these angels.

In both the Hindu religion and in Buddhism, a group of higher *devas* could be likened to angels. The Hindus believe they are responsible for controlling much of the natural world under the supreme god Lord Vishnu, while in Buddhism the *devas* are more powerful and longer-lived than humans, and closer to the divine, as well as being ranked in a hierarchy.

Angelic beings in different cultures

We have already mentioned some pre-Christian divine messengers of the Assyrians, Greeks and Romans. Such beings are also found in Sumerian, Babylonian, Persian and Egyptian cultures. These traditions often demonstrated a search for balance similar to the way the Ancient Egyptians viewed their gods, which was more as superior beings who could help and protect humans and who

could be petitioned to intercede with the highest authorities. The idea of the angelic oracle, which we have touched on already, is resonant of the Egyptian goddess Ma'at, who represented justice and truth. After death, Ma'at and Osiris, the god of death, weighed the heart of the deceased in a balance against Ma'at's feather of truth, while 42 gods or goddesses asked questions about how that person had lived their life. If the heart was light because the person had led a good life, then they gained eternal life. If the heart was heavy, then it was eaten by the goddess Ammut.

Many Wiccans believe in angels as a positive life force that connects the inner soul with the deeper reality of spirituality around us. It is the link with the angels that is our link with the life force itself.

The angel within

It is clear that, however we define angels and whatever our spiritual beliefs, their goodness and spiritual purity are common factors, along with the link to something higher or better than ourselves.

This inescapable link between angels, inner purity and spirituality is fundamental. It may be because, at our best, we try to mirror God's goodness in a small way. This holds good for those who are religious – whatever religion they belong to – because angels are on a closer plane to the divine. But it also opens the possibility that anyone with an open mind can aspire to be 'angelic': pure and good, spiritual, protective and caring, an energy or force for good that links to whatever divine concept you believe in.

Such an energy resides in our innermost being, our angel oracle, ready to be harnessed for the good of others and ourselves. You can call it your conscience, your better self, or the spark of the divine, but it is that spark we are trying to ignite in this book.

Visual representations of angels

In the Bible, angels are always referred to as masculine and I have followed that tradition in this book. I have chosen to use the masculine pronoun for ease of reading and because it seems most appropriate. However, the focus of this book is primarily on angels as energy permeating your subconscious, which means every manifestation will be unique to each individual. Angels are variously represented in art and literature as both male and female: traditional sources favour the former; modern, often Wiccan,

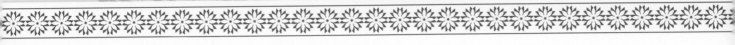

sources prefer the latter. But they are usually androgynous: tall and strong in a masculine way, but with a striking beauty and softness of expression that lends them a femininity. Combining the best qualities of males and females is important because it demonstrates that there are good qualities in all of us regardless of gender or, indeed, any other distinguishing features. Gender itself is irrelevant because it is transcended by spiritual goodness.

The symbol of angels' role as messengers is their wings, which are usually feathered and always muscular, powerful and as tall as the angel himself. The angels' association with God is symbolized by a halo, a ring of light energy above their head, and they are often seen emanating light or surrounded by an aura, which is appropriate, as they are beings made of light. Clothed in flowing robes, timeless and of no particular culture, they are associated with an intense white light as a symbol of their purity. Where colour is introduced – in their robes or sometimes their aura – it is part of the symbolism of the angel himself. Thus Michael, the warrior, is associated with gold, while Raphael, the healer, is often seen emanating a green light. Similarly, many symbols are associated with angels. For example, Michael carries a sword and Raphael a staff or caduceus.

Over the centuries, angels have been represented in every conceivable artistic style and medium, from pencil to marble to 200 tonnes of steel. Such representations have certainly influenced popular culture and people's imaginations, as the images that emerge are based on earlier concepts which artists have assimilated, but every new work adds to our conscious or subconscious image of what an angel should look like.

It is remarkable that across a broad timeframe and throughout global culture, angelic features have remained so similar. While other symbols have evolved, the figure of an angel appears to be fixed in our collective consciousness. There are so many images of angels that it would be impossible to find a representative selection, but any assortment will illustrate how our imaginations have depicted the angelic form with striking consistency. For example, images of powerful outstretched wings can be found as readily in fourteenth-century Italian sculpture as in modern Asian decoration, while some art deco representations evoke Ancient Egyptian carvings. I think this is a positive sign which indicates we know what goodness is and can recognize it and give it shape. Visual representations of angels show us that we can find ways to link to the divine, within or beyond ourselves.

The angelic hierarchy

In Christian tradition there is a hierarchy of angels, established in the 5th century by Dionysus: it consists of three choirs, or triads, gradually moving further away from the divine.

Nearest to God are the seraphim, cherubim and thrones, or just the former two in the Old Testament. The word seraphim comes from the Hebrew verb *seraph*, meaning 'to burn'. Seraphim are often associated with fire – perhaps because they are beings of pure light, or are closest to the brilliance of God and the highest order of his angels, or perhaps because their own light is so intense that no human could stand to look at them without combusting. They are responsible for world peace and the healing of the planet. The cherubim are the guardians of the stars, who transmit light and knowledge through the universe. The thrones represent justice and protect nations struggling under oppressive regimes.

On the next level are the dominions, the virtues and the powers, the link between the upper and lower choirs. Demanding the highest standards, the dominions concentrate on putting spiritual principles into practice on Earth. The virtues focus on nature and the positive energies of the natural world. The powers are warrior angels concerned with life and death.

The final triad is made up of the principalities, who are the teachers, the archangels and the angels. These last two work closest to humankind and commune between God and humans – it is the angels and archangels who are the subject of this book.

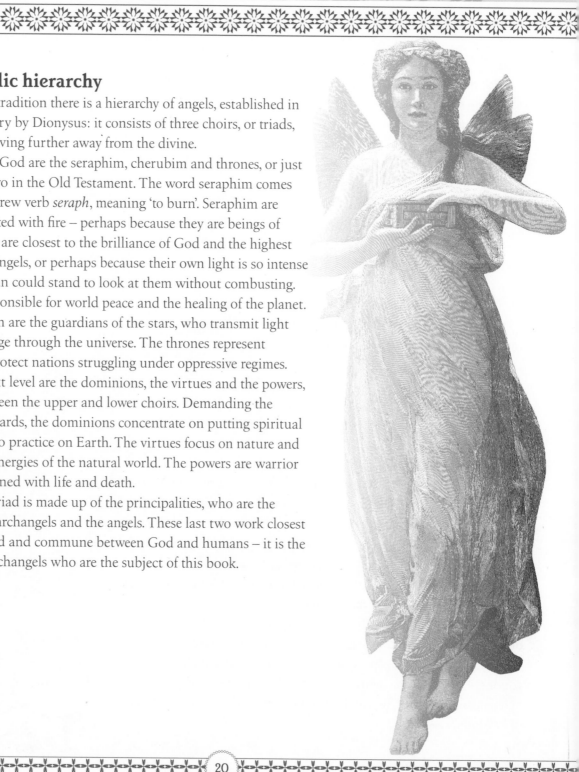

The Angel of the North

Antony Gormley's Angel of the North stands 20 metres high on a hillside near Gateshead, northern England, dominating the skyline with its 54 metre wingspan and towering over the thousands who come to see it. Angelic power is instantly recognizable in its vast, muscular structure, but the gentle forward slant of the wings also expresses the protective role of the angel.

Andrew Gormley explained: 'People are always asking, why an angel? The only response I can give is that no one has ever seen one and we need to keep imagining them. The angel has three functions – firstly a historic one to remind us that below this site coal miners worked in the dark for two hundred years, secondly to grasp hold of the future, expressing our transition from the industrial to the information age, and lastly to be a focus for our hopes and fears – a sculpture is an evolving thing.

'The hilltop site is important and has the feeling of being a megalithic mound. When you think of the mining that was done underneath the site, there is a poetic resonance. Men worked beneath the surface in the dark. Now in the light, there is a celebration of this industry. The face will not have individual features. The effect of the piece is in the alertness, the awareness of space and the gesture of the wings – they are not flat, they're about 3.5 degrees forward and give a sense of embrace.'

Who are the angels?

Since there are countless angels in the third triad who act as a bridge between humans and the divine, this book focuses on a representative selection whose characteristics can help us build our own bridge to the spiritual plane.

> 'Millions of spiritual creatures walk the earth Unseen, both when we wake and when we sleep.'
>
> *Paradise Lost*, John Milton (1608–1674)

Selecting our angels

The angels in the third choir, led by the archangels, are those who have authority over the natural world and are therefore those who are potentially able to support and guide us. Mentioned frequently in both the Old and New Testaments, the number of angels is generally, although not universally, fixed, and so massive (14th-century scholars would tell you it is over 300,000,000) that it is impossible to study them in their entirety in a book of this kind. Our focus will therefore be on a small group of the archangels.

Each angel represents an archetype and has specific virtues, or characteristics, and a tightly defined sphere of influence. By choosing a specific group of angels, we can link them with the various strands of spiritual energy we need to cope with the challenges of life, so that at least one of them can be called on in most circumstances in which you find yourself.

However, it is not easy to decide which angels to study. Although angels are mentioned in the Bible, they are rarely referenced by name, so while the three primary archangels are easy to identify and are known by the familiar names of Michael, Gabriel and Raphael, it is less easy to be specific about the other angels and archangels.

This is not simply because they are not named in the scriptures – they are named in many other texts. The reason it is difficult to be specific is because consistency cannot be found. The same angel may have as many as eight or nine different names, some of which are variations of spelling, such as Anael and Aniyel, while others may be completely different, such as Simiel and Haniel (and these are just four of many names given to the same angel!). It is therefore extremely difficult – if not impossible – for anyone but a scholar to be sure that they are talking about the same angel.

The descriptions of each angel's primary qualities may also be variously defined in different texts. For example, you may find Cassiel associated with temperance rather than tears, or Camael with joy rather than courage. In most cases, each angel has a broader remit than one would initially think and it is quite easy to establish the links between the qualities they are said to represent. Bringing comfort to ease sadness involves restoring the balance of life, using temperance to mitigate extremes. Giving you courage to make your way through adversity can lead you back to joy.

So how is it possible to select just a small group of angels to call upon in a straightforward and practical book designed for self-improvement? Is it not a fairly arbitrary choice and one that could be challenged? The simple answer is 'yes', but the question is not really relevant to this particular book.

The archangels we have chosen to feature are among the most commonly known and therefore the names and characteristics tend to be less difficult to fathom. Readers will most likely recognize angel characteristics

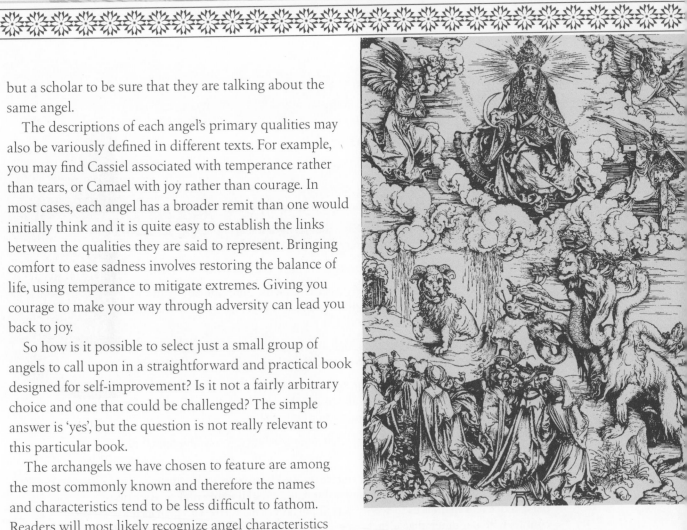

from earlier reading or follow up their interest in other books without finding the transition blocked by nomenclature. These archangels may well be found with slightly different names or qualities elsewhere, but their definitions should be broadly consistent.

While there are known to be seven archangels, mentioned in Revelation, surrounding the throne of God, extending that group to twelve allows us to use an angel to represent archetypes, a carefully selected range of qualities that we need to help us make the best of our lives, to find peace, happiness and spiritual enlightenment. Each archetype represents a collection of positive qualities that are of immense value. You may choose to call these archetypes by different angel names or you may make contact with other angels when you reach out to the angelic oracle, but the spiritual quality and the benefit will remain.

Having a name for the angel you call upon will give your invocation more power and direction, and it will be far more likely to succeed, even if it is another angel who responds.

The archangels of the angel oracle

Below are the twelve archangels chosen to represent the spiritual virtues to which we aspire:

* ❋ ANAEL The angel Anael brings us calm to help us cope with what life throws at us.

* ❋ CAMAEL When we feel we do not have the strength to carry on, Camael can bring us courage in adversity and positive energy to enable us to cope.

* ❋ CASSIEL Cassiel, the angel of compassion, brings comfort when it is most needed.

* ❋ GABRIEL The archangel most closely associated with communication and with understanding ourselves, other people and relationships, Gabriel shows us how to find the best in ourselves – the heart of our creativity.

* ❋ METATRON Metatron is related to logical thought and organization, so is called upon to help us when we want to broaden our outlook, to grow and to learn.

* ❋ MICHAEL The leader of the warrior angels who fight evil, Michael offers protection and helps us to keep those we love safe. Michael is also known as the angel of miracles, who can inspire us to strive to optimize our potential.

* ❋ RAPHAEL Raphael is the angelic healer, bringing balance and well-being, both physical and spiritual.

* ❋ RAZIEL Possessed of all knowledge in Heaven and Earth, Raziel has deep, unconscious wisdom. He helps us understand our most fundamental needs, brings perspective and enables us to see what is important to us. Raziel can help us make contact with our inner angel oracle so we can start the process of spiritual growth.

* ❋ SACHIEL In control of the four elements and bringing abundance and prosperity, Sachiel teaches us to be thankful for the blessings in our lives and to appreciate the joy to be found in small things.

* ❋ SANDALPHON Understanding of other people and our relationships is fostered by Sandalphon, who reveals the route our path through this life should take.

* ❋ URIEL Uriel represents change and fosters the ability to adapt to circumstances as they evolve.

* ❋ ZADKIEL The soul of generosity, Zadkiel is the ideal spiritual companion for life's special celebrations.

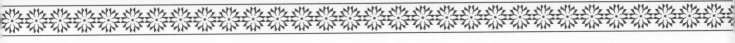

Correspondences

Correspondences are familiar from Wiccan tradition but appear less frequently in a religious context. The term refers to the linking of characteristics associated with a primary concept. On the subject of angels, the blurring of the boundaries between religion and culture mean that specific angels are often associated with many other features, including:

- ✳ planets and zodiac signs
- ✳ seasons, months, days, and times of the day and night
- ✳ elements
- ✳ crystals
- ✳ colours and the colours of the aura
- ✳ oils and fragrances
- ✳ herbs and other plants
- ✳ chakras
- ✳ numbers
- ✳ symbols

While looking at the spiritual characteristics of our chosen angels, we will also discuss their most prominent correspondences. When we come to call upon our angels in later chapters, these correspondences will help us to create an atmosphere conducive to making spiritual contact by timing our meditation, using candles or incense, appropriate chants, music or colours.

Not every angel has developed associations in all areas. Where a particular correspondence has not been listed, it indicates there is no strong association in that area.

Anael — 'the grace of God'

One of the seven angels who stand before God, Anael is an angel who surrounds us with love and healing, bringing an atmosphere of calm in which we can flourish and find our own way to cope with the stresses of everyday life. To do this, we must feel confident and secure – that we are valued and appreciated. Anael helps us to recognize and take responsibility for the things we can change and to acknowledge those we cannot. Few things are more stressful than feeling we must change something over which we have no control. But we can control ourselves, our reactions to other people and the circumstances in which we find ourselves. So we can start making changes where it is possible to do so.

Associated with the planet Venus, the evening star, Anael is also concerned with human sexuality and physical love. If you need to behave graciously – at an important event, for example – Anael's energies may help you.

A common representation of Anael is an angel surrounded by the green light of healing and the rose-pink light of love. Often seen holding flowers, especially roses, he has delicate features and shining silver wings.

ASSOCIATIONS

❋ **Planet**   Venus
❋ **Zodiac**   Capricorn
❋ **Month**   December
❋ **Day**   Friday
❋ **Element**   Water
❋ **Colours**   Rose pink, green
❋ **Crystals**   Pink: calcite, rose quartz
                  Green: aventurine,
                  chrysoprase, fluorite, jasper
❋ **Metal**   Weathered copper
❋ **Plants**   Apple blossom, hibiscus,
                  rose, valerian
❋ **Symbol**   Rose

Camael — 'the one who sees God'

Camael is one of the seven angels who stand before God. He brings courage and the strength to cope with trials and tribulations, especially when we feel as though we are running out of energy and find it hard to keep going. Camael helps us to overcome our enemies. He is sometimes said to be the angel who appeared to comfort Jesus in the garden of Gethsemane (although that angel is usually identified as Gabriel). Camael shows us how to maintain our courage in adversity by reminding us that joy and contentment can be found in the smallest of things. He is sometimes called the angel of joy.

Another way Camael helps us to cope is by showing us that we can forgive ourselves for not having all the answers. If we can love ourselves, with all our faults, then we are less likely to blame or criticize others. For this reason, Camael is associated with tolerance and with justice. He helps us to clear up misunderstandings, resolve difficulties in relationships and gain a positive but balanced outlook.

Camael's signature colour of red is featured in representations in his robes, wings or aura. He is also said to appear as a leopard sitting on a rock.

ASSOCIATIONS

* **Planet** Mars
* **Day** Tuesday
* **Element** Fire
* **Colour** Red
* **Crystals** Bloodstone, carnelian, garnet, jasper
* **Metals** Iron and steel
* **Plants and oils** Ginger, geranium, mint, neroli, parsley, tangerine
* **Number** Nine
* **Symbol** Leopard sitting on a rock

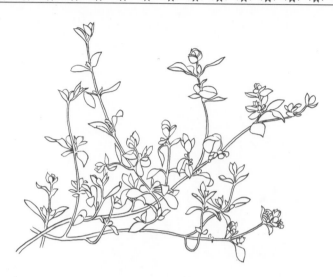

Cassiel — 'speed of God'

Cassiel, the angel of compassion, is known as the angel who weeps silently. He brings us comfort in times of grief, loss and heartache and shares our sorrow. He shows us that with patience and fortitude we can restore the natural balance. His virtues are the acceptance of what is and what must be, and the wisdom to understand.

Often appearing as bearded, Cassiel's colours of black and indigo are seen in the flames emitting from his halo, and in his dark robes. He is sometimes shown riding a dragon.

ASSOCIATIONS

* **Planet**   Saturn
* **Day**   Saturday
* **Element**   Earth
* **Colours**   Indigo, black
* **Crystals**   Indigo: azurite, iolite
  Black: obsidian, onyx
* **Metal**   Lead
* **Plants**   Clary sage, cypress, marjoram, patchouli, violet
* **Chakra**   Balancing all chakras
* **Number**   Three
* **Symbols**   Dove, dragon

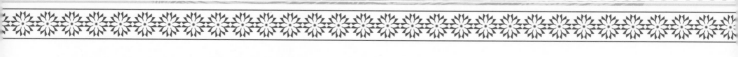

Gabriel — 'God is my strength'

Gabriel is one of the best-known angels. Along with Michael, he is the highest-ranking angel in Judeo-Christian and Islamic lore (these are the only two angels named in the Old Testament). Gabriel is one of the seven angels who stand before God. His virtues are wide-ranging, as he presides over death, resurrection, mercy and vengeance. He is also renowned as the angel of annunciation and revelation, who brought the news to the Virgin Mary that she was to bear a son. Gabriel is said to have dictated the Koran to Mohammed, and to Muslims he represents truth.

Understanding the truth about ourselves inspires us to maintain our integrity, develop our strengths and mitigate our weaknesses. As the guardian of Paradise, Gabriel gives us the strength to reach for that ultimate goal. He also inspires us to develop our individual gifts and share them with others. Part of his remit is also to control and stave off destructive behaviour, and search within ourselves for the most positive energies. Gabriel's energies can help us to overcome the fear of procrastination, and may enhance our dreams and further our aspirations.

The moon or a lantern are often shown in depictions of Gabriel. The lilies associated with him, usually in depictions of the Annunciation, symbolize purity and are associated with the Virgin Mary.

ASSOCIATIONS

* **Planet**   Moon
* **Zodiac**   Aquarius
* **Direction**   West
* **Season**   Autumn
* **Month**   January
* **Day**   Monday
* **Time**   Sunset
* **Element**   Water
* **Colours**   Silver, white
* **Crystals**   Moonstone, milky quartz, pearl
* **Metal**   Silver
* **Plants**   Eucalyptus, jasmine, lilac, lily, myrrh, sandalwood, white rose
* **Chakra**   Sacral
* **Number**   Eight
* **Symbols**   Lilies, lantern

Metatron — 'on the throne next to the divine'

A fundamental link between the human and the divine, the angel Metatron was once human and known as the prophet Enoch. Some occult sources describe him as the brother of Sandalphon. As the heavenly scribe, Metatron's virtues include understanding, spiritual knowledge, logical thought and organization. He helps us when we want to broaden our outlook, to grow and to learn. He is said to be the guardian of the tree of life.

Metatron understands the blueprints to every life form; these are recorded in Metatron's Cube, a matrix of all life. The Cube contains all the maps and plans you might need on every step of your life journey, giving you the required knowledge to expand both intellectually and spiritually. By opening the doors of the mind to spiritual awareness, Metatron can be particularly influential with young people and his energies support anything to do with youth.

When he ascended to heaven, Metatron became a spirit of fire with innumerable eyes and thirty-six pairs of wings, and he is sometimes shown as a column of fire. He is often described as the tallest and youngest of the angels.

ASSOCIATIONS

❈ **Planet** Pluto
❈ **Direction** North
❈ **Day** Sunday
❈ **Element** Fire
❈ **Colours** Maroon, white
❈ **Crystals** Maroon: aventurine, jasper, selenite, sardonyx
White: calcite, crystal quartz, howlite, kunzite, selenite
❈ **Plants** Carnation, cedar, frankincense, juniper, myrrh
❈ **Chakras** Crown and heart
❈ **Number** One
❈ **Symbol** Tree of Life

Michael — 'he who is like God'

Along with Gabriel, Michael is the supreme angel of all religions and one of the seven angels who stand before the throne of God. He may have been the angel who vanquished Lucifer and expelled him from Heaven, and who told Mary of her impending death.

His primary virtue is as the leader of the warrior angels designated to fight evil and maintain justice and integrity. Strength and supreme goodness are his to bestow. Michael protects us from negative energies and inspires us to protect others. As a commander of angels, he can help with issues of leadership and confidence, offering his strength and protection. As the benevolent angel of death, he has the power to lead humankind to eternal light, or judge us for our failings. Michael is also the angel of miracles who can inspire us to greater heights of creativity. He gives us courage to pursue the truth, and the energy to help us face and solve our problems.

Michael oversees the natural world, from the weather and agriculture to nature's eco-systems. He can influence the abundance and prosperity of our surroundings and our livelihoods. When he wept upon telling the fallen angels about the Flood, his tears turned to precious stones of great value.

As the warrior angel, Michael is shown with golden wings and halo, red and gold armour and with a sword and shield. He frequently carries a banner with a red cross, wears a blue cloak and holds the scales of justice in his hand. He is sometimes seen killing a dragon, prefiguring the image of St George.

ASSOCIATIONS

* **Planet**   Sun
* **Direction** South
* **Season**   Summer
* **Day**   Sunday
* **Time**   Noon
* **Element**   Fire
* **Colours**   Gold, yellow, blue
* **Crystals**   Gold: amber, citrine, topaz
                 Blue: lapis lazuli, sapphire
* **Metal**   Gold
* **Plants**   Bergamot, chamomile, cinnamon, eucalyptus, eyebright, frankincense, lemon, lemon balm, mistletoe, myrrh, rosemary, sage, St John's wort, sunflower
* **Chakras**   Throat and solar plexus
* **Number**   Six
* **Symbols**   Sword, sun

Raphael – 'God has healed'

Raphael is one of the archangels mentioned by name in the Bible and he consistently appears in texts as one of the seven primary archangels. While there are disagreements about the virtues of all the other archangels, every source designates Raphael as the angel of healing. Raphael healed Jacob's wounds after he wrestled with an angel. Raphael also rippled the waters at the pool of Bethesda, where bathers were subsequently healed.

In the *Book of Tobias*, Raphael visits Tobit, a devoted Jewish man, who has asked God to let him die because his blindness renders his life unbearable. At the same time, a woman called Sarah makes the same request because she has lost seven husbands, each of them dying on her wedding night before the marriage was consummated. Raphael brings Tobit's son, Tobias, into contact with Sarah and they fall in love. Tobias makes an ointment that cures his father's blindness and drives out the demons causing Sarah's problems.

This story demonstrates how angels act as a catalyst on our actions. Tobias solves the problems, with guidance and inspiration from the angel.

Raphael's healing powers are not confined to physical matters. Spiritual health, well-being and happiness are also part of his remit. He helps us ward off negative influences that might affect our spiritual or physical health. He may encourage us to take measures to avoid catching a virus, or defend ourselves against the ravages of modern life. He may help us heal a rocky relationship, overcome a sense of grief or mend a friendship.

Other areas of influence include travel and joyful meetings, so Raphael can also be called upon to bring his energies to celebrations and festivals.

Surrounded by rays of green light, Raphael is traditionally depicted carrying a staff, the symbol of a pilgrim or traveller, and holding a golden phial of medicine and a bag of food for travellers.

ASSOCIATIONS

❋ **Planet** Mercury
❋ **Direction** East
❋ **Season** Spring
❋ **Day** Wednesday
❋ **Time** Dawn
❋ **Element** Air
❋ **Colours** Green, or sometimes yellow
❋ **Crystals** Green: aventurine, beryl, chrysoprase, emerald, jade, malachite
Yellow: citrine, honey calcite, fluorite, jasper
❋ **Metals** Aluminium, mercury
❋ **Plants** Bergamot, geranium, lavender, lily of the valley, parsley, pine, rose, sandalwood, thyme, valerian
❋ **Chakra** Heart
❋ **Numbers** Eight, Six
❋ **Symbol** Caduceus

Raziel – 'secret of God'

Raziel is known as the angel of mysteries because he has access to a deep, unconscious wisdom that reveals all earthly and heavenly knowledge. He has the power to impart elements of the secrets hidden within the esoteric book of angels, a compendium of all spiritual wisdom.

Raziel inspires us to look beyond the superficial and examine the deeper meanings in life, to understand life's mystery and not fear our psychic abilities. He helps us focus on what is fundamentally important to us and, by doing so, allows us to move forward with confidence in our innate abilities.

With this sense of perspective and good judgement comes an intuitive understanding of how to behave in order to put other people at ease and in touch with their deeper, unconscious understanding.

Sometimes illustrated as semi-opaque, because he deals with psychic and mystic knowledge, Raziel is clothed in flowing robes of misty grey or dark green. His light is subtle, in contrast to angels like Michael, and his impact is deep and intense.

ASSOCIATIONS

❃	**Planet**	Uranus
❃	**Day**	Saturday
❃	**Time**	Twilight
❃	**Element**	Air
❃	**Colours**	Grey, dark green
❃	**Crystals**	Grey: fossils, smoky quartz
		Green: opal, peridot, sardonyx, tourmaline
❃	**Metal**	Lead
❃	**Plants and oils**	Ambergris, cedar, myrrh
❃	**Number**	One
❃	**Chakra**	Brow

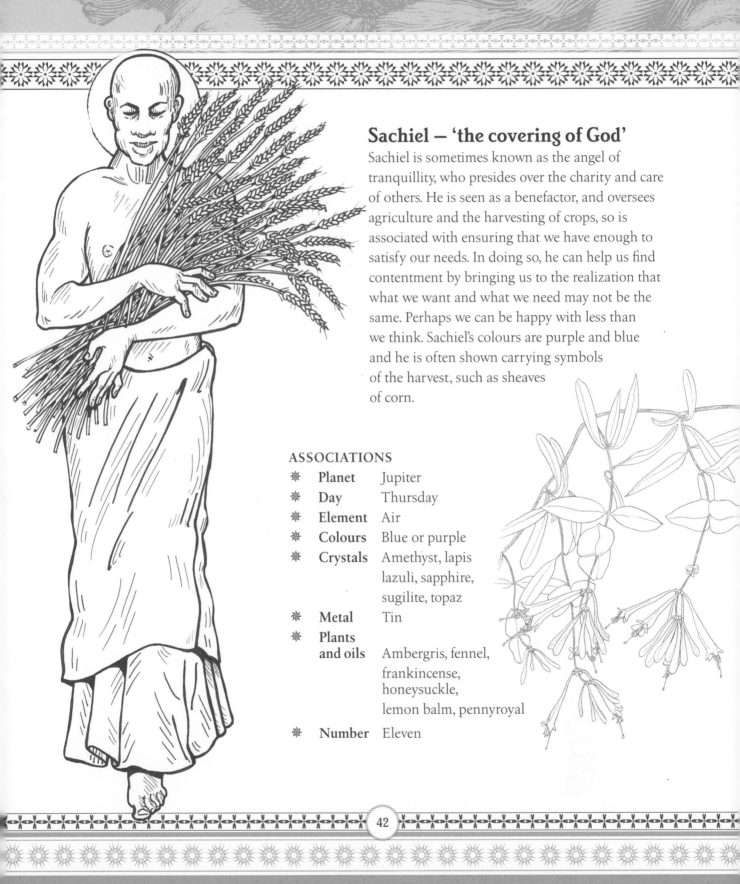

Sachiel — 'the covering of God'

Sachiel is sometimes known as the angel of tranquillity, who presides over the charity and care of others. He is seen as a benefactor, and oversees agriculture and the harvesting of crops, so is associated with ensuring that we have enough to satisfy our needs. In doing so, he can help us find contentment by bringing us to the realization that what we want and what we need may not be the same. Perhaps we can be happy with less than we think. Sachiel's colours are purple and blue and he is often shown carrying symbols of the harvest, such as sheaves of corn.

ASSOCIATIONS

* **Planet** Jupiter
* **Day** Thursday
* **Element** Air
* **Colours** Blue or purple
* **Crystals** Amethyst, lapis lazuli, sapphire, sugilite, topaz
* **Metal** Tin
* **Plants and oils** Ambergris, fennel, frankincense, honeysuckle, lemon balm, pennyroyal
* **Number** Eleven

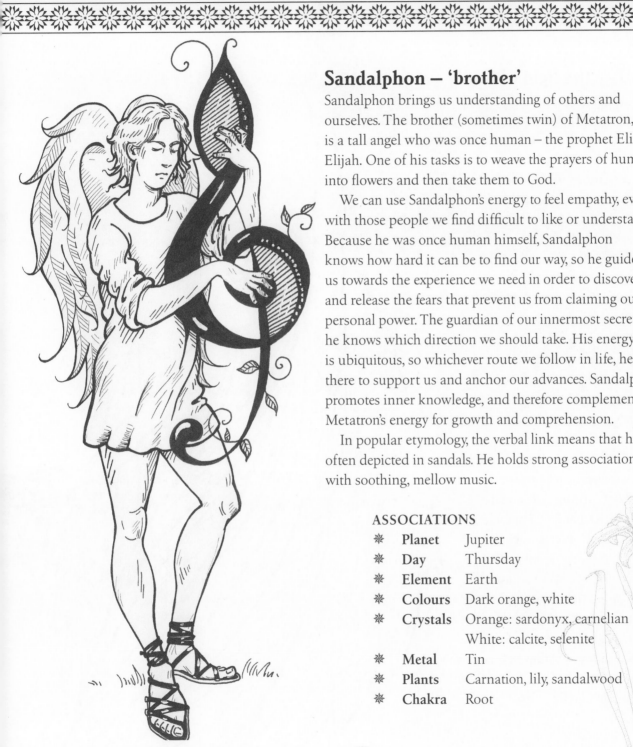

Sandalphon — 'brother'

Sandalphon brings us understanding of others and ourselves. The brother (sometimes twin) of Metatron, he is a tall angel who was once human – the prophet Elias or Elijah. One of his tasks is to weave the prayers of humans into flowers and then take them to God.

We can use Sandalphon's energy to feel empathy, even with those people we find difficult to like or understand. Because he was once human himself, Sandalphon knows how hard it can be to find our way, so he guides us towards the experience we need in order to discover and release the fears that prevent us from claiming our personal power. The guardian of our innermost secrets, he knows which direction we should take. His energy is ubiquitous, so whichever route we follow in life, he is there to support us and anchor our advances. Sandalphon promotes inner knowledge, and therefore complements Metatron's energy for growth and comprehension.

In popular etymology, the verbal link means that he is often depicted in sandals. He holds strong associations with soothing, mellow music.

ASSOCIATIONS

❈	**Planet**	Jupiter
❈	**Day**	Thursday
❈	**Element**	Earth
❈	**Colours**	Dark orange, white
❈	**Crystals**	Orange: sardonyx, carnelian
		White: calcite, selenite
❈	**Metal**	Tin
❈	**Plants**	Carnation, lily, sandalwood
❈	**Chakra**	Root

Uriel — 'the light of God'

Uriel, the angel of the light of God, is a force for change and transformation, overseeing the creation of new materials and the cycle of life through birth, growth, death and rebirth. As change is one of life's only certainties, we can use Uriel's help to embrace it and retain a balanced view of the process of life. This will encourage us to adapt to circumstances as they evolve. Uriel's strengthening and stabilizing energy gives us a firm foundation so that we can develop our most positive talents. With his gift of unconditional love, he brings the opportunity to transform lower energies to a higher vibration so that we can overcome our baser nature and become truer to our spiritual selves. Uriel helps to change negative energies and dispel destructive emotions, and he offers protection from harm.

Not surprisingly, Uriel is associated with alchemy, the process of turning base metal into gold. Alchemy is a miracle humans have never mastered – except in fiction – but we can try to achieve it in our spiritual lives.

Because Uriel is the angel of transformation, which necessitates sharp insight, he can also foster psychic abilities. Making a link to him is the perfect way to get in touch with our inner angel oracle.

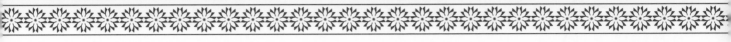

Uriel is depicted with an open hand holding a flame, dressed in flame-coloured robes, with red light emitting from his halo. He sometimes carries a scroll.

ASSOCIATIONS

✳ **Planet** Mars
✳ **Zodiac** Libra
✳ **Direction** North
✳ **Season** Winter
✳ **Month** September
✳ **Day** Saturday
✳ **Time** Midnight
✳ **Element** Earth
✳ **Colour** Reddish brown
✳ **Crystals** Haematite, rutilated quartz, tiger's eye
✳ **Metals** Brass or burnished gold
✳ **Plants** Basil, bergamot, chamomile, clary sage, dill, fennel, ginger, juniper, lemon, sandalwood
✳ **Chakra** Solar plexus
✳ **Number** Five
✳ **Symbols** Lightning, a scroll

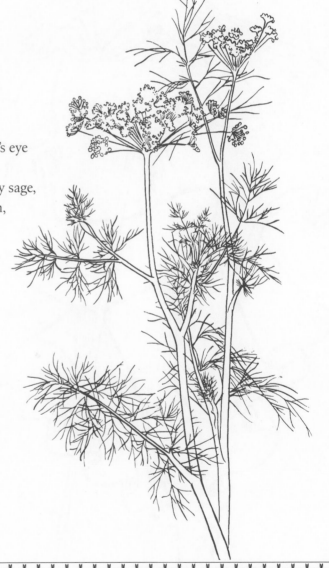

Zadkiel – 'God's blessing'

Zadkiel is the angel of the righteousness of God. Often designated as one of the seven archangels who stand before God, he is the soul of generosity, the ideal spiritual companion for life's celebrations. Imbued with benevolence, forgiveness and tolerance for the weakness of others, Zadkiel is the angel of compassion who wants us to see the best in life, to celebrate abundance and success. Fairness and a just distribution of resources are crucial attributes of his, and his energy can help us view others with compassion and understanding rather than judgement. His energy is about balance and harmony, bringing all life elements together in the praise of God.

Zadkiel is the angel who uses his power of joy to heal troubled minds. He can be especially effective in helping young people who are depressed or afraid.

Zadkiel's light is usually depicted as blue, as are his wings and robes. As a warrior of Michael's army, he carries a dagger and a white standard.

ASSOCIATIONS

- ❋ **Planet**   Jupiter
- ❋ **Day**   Thursday
- ❋ **Element**   Air
- ❋ **Colour**   Sky blue
- ❋ **Crystals**   Blue celeste, chalcedony, blue howlite, lapis lazuli, blue quartz, sapphire, turquoise
- ❋ **Metals**   Tin, zinc
- ❋ **Plants**   Arnica, bergamot, borage, cedarwood, frankincense, ginseng, lemon balm, neroli, nutmeg, rosemary, sage, ylang ylang
- ❋ **Chakra**   Crown
- ❋ **Numbers**   Four, twelve
- ❋ **Symbols**   Dagger, white standard

Angelic guidance

The exercises in later chapters each focus on one of the twelve archangels in this chapter, but more as concepts than single beings. For example, if you call on Raphael to help in healing some distress in your life, your call may be answered by any number of lesser angels who can minister to you equally well. At some point you may discover that you have a guardian angel who is always there for you whatever your problem. The chapter on guardian angels (see page 199) contains the names of other angels you may like to investigate. In each case, the process is about finding your own, unique path.

Calling Out to the Angels

Whether we believe they are
external spiritual beings or a part of
our deepest subconscious, angels do exist
and can help us. If communing with angels
— or simply tuning in to our angel oracle —
achieves the objective of making us better, happier and more fulfilled, then it is a spiritual
power for good. That has to be a sound enough reason for finding the best techniques to
help you make contact.

In some cases, people have experienced angelic encounters in the most traumatic
moments; when they were in most need, angels came to help them out of a dire situation.

We can open ourselves up to angelic influence in the simplest of ways: through
relaxation, dreaming, meditation or simply by being more open minded.

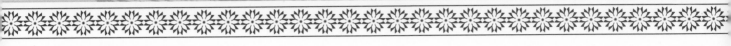

Spiritual guidance from your angel oracle

There is no end to the ways angels can influence our lives and it may be in the most surprising, or unexpected, circumstances that we feel their influence. Whether we seek their help by calling on them, or whether they come to us apparently unbidden to offer their support and protection in a crisis, angels are our link with the divine. They put us in touch with what is finest in our nature so that we can make the best of whatever circumstances we find ourselves in.

It could be that our angel oracle helps us make a difficult decision, protects us from harm, or simply brings us joy. In any event, it is a lifting of the spirit.

To achieve this, it is necessary to get in touch with what you really want to be doing with your life. You are the person who knows best what is right for you, and you understand that feeling deep in your unconscious. Establishing a link with this intuitive knowledge is the key to finding your link with the angels.

'We tend to forget that happiness doesn't come as a result of getting something we don't have but rather of recognizing and appreciating what we do have.'

Friedrich Koenig (1774–1833), inventor

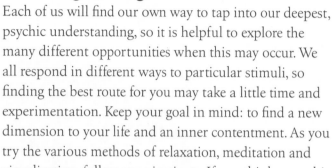

Touching the angels

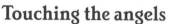

Each of us will find our own way to tap into our deepest, psychic understanding, so it is helpful to explore the many different opportunities when this may occur. We all respond in different ways to particular stimuli, so finding the best route for you may take a little time and experimentation. Keep your goal in mind: to find a new dimension to your life and an inner contentment. As you try the various methods of relaxation, meditation and visualization, follow your instincts. If you think something sounds silly, don't do it. If you have a different idea you think might work, then try it. This is your journey and only you can decide what is right.

In particular, the right physical stimuli are important because they will create the appropriate mood for your inner journey. Remember that it is your personal journey, so be guided by what feels right to you. If yellow crystals are suggested as a correspondence but you find them too harsh, simply look for something you feel is appropriate and use that instead, preferably keeping within the general area of the original suggestion.

And you will succeed. You may see a falling feather, experience a rush or joy or a moment of inspiration or understanding. Your role in life may become clearer. If you call on the angels in a genuine and sincere spirit, then help will be available.

How can angels help you?

If we open our minds and shake up our senses, we can find angels even in the most unlikely places — angels to brighten a bad day. Or we can access a more potent spiritual dimension to link us with powers beyond ourselves.

Life as we know it

Most of us have increasingly busy lives and spend our time earning a living, looking after a home, perhaps raising a family. There is always something to do, a task that we can't put off any longer, or perhaps something we really need to make the time to complete. Everyday life takes up every minute of our time.

So what happened to the benefits of all the labour- and time-saving devices invented over the last generation that were supposed to make life so much easier? Teenagers have never known life without mobile phones, the internet, email, air travel available to everyone, or video conferencing. But when people who are now only in their late 50s were going to school, TVs were black-and-white, refrigerators were by no means in all homes, and there were still telephone switchboard operators – you picked up your home telephone, waited for the operator, and told her the number you wanted! Some people had a 'party line' shared with next door, which meant that they might pick up their phone and find the neighbours chatting away. Central heating, washing machines, dishwashers, freezers, vacuum cleaners, tumble driers and food processors are all relatively recent innovations that take the hard work out of chores at home. Now we have the luxury of all this extra time that we used to spend sweeping, chopping and daily shopping, what are we

> 'The voyage to discovery is not in seeking new landscapes, but in having new eyes.'
> Marcel Proust (1871–1922), writer and critic

doing with it? Clearly we are not using it to find better ways to relax because we are generally much more stressed than previous generations. It seems that every technological advance opens up another avenue that must be explored, raises the attainment bar higher and makes us want even more material things. And although we are more technologically savvy – perhaps more street-wise and sophisticated – we are no more contented with our lives. In fact, simple contentment may have been the biggest casualty of progress.

Listening to the little angels

There are two major problems with this way of living. If we are so busy and preoccupied that we focus more on what we are supposed to be doing next, rather than what we are doing now, then we throw away the opportunity to appreciate the positive elements of the present. They may only be the smallest details, but if we give them our full attention for just a few extra seconds, they can bring a totally disproportionate enjoyment. In addition to this, if we are only concerned with the physical and material world, we lose the link to our spiritual dimension, to our inner angel.

When we look at these two lost opportunities, it becomes clear that they are, in fact, one and the same thing. If we have lost our sense of balance to such an extent that we are not in touch with what really matters, how can we expect to truly appreciate what is going on around us? But if we can tap into our angel oracle – that part of us that knows what is best for us, that gives us a sense of priorities and helps us find something worthwhile within and beyond our normal selves – then we can bring a spiritual, angelic dimension into our lives. And what an enriching experience that can be!

We are all distracted by the 'what if?' and 'what's next?' questions. But if that is our permanent emotional state, our senses begin to close down. Turning in on ourselves in this way is negative because human contact and contact with the natural world is invigorating. If we are always looking for the next stimulus, we will not see the one in front of us. Let's look at a couple of examples.

You are hanging out the washing – you don't have much time because you need to get to work, do the shopping, ring your mum and remember to pick up the dry-cleaning – when suddenly a bird flies down and lands in front of you. The temptation is to flick the next item of washing to hang on the line, but what a missed opportunity that would be. Don't ignore the little bird. It may not have the splendour of an angel but it might have been sent to tell you to slow down, to stop and look. Take just a minute to look at his beady eye and pretty plumage. This won't make any difference to your journey time, it is not going to mean that nothing else gets done, but it could give you a wonderful lift to carry you through the rest of the day.

You are in slow-moving traffic and two lanes are filtering together. You are stressed and not inclined to let the car next to you go in front because, if you don't, you could just catch the lights. But the young girl in the back seat gives you such a beaming smile that you drop back to second place – and still go through on green. Was she a little angel sent to calm you down? It's highly unlikely, but why not treat these seemingly insignificant incidents as manifestations of the power of goodness and beauty to make our lives better, more meaningful and more contented?

Linking us with our humanity

Such encounters are a reminder that we are all part of humanity and if we feed into that collective it can be of immense benefit to all of us. The Wiccan principle states that what we give out comes back threefold. If your outlook is positive, that can only be good news.

If we allow ourselves a little time for reflection so that we discover our inner angel, it can help us to realize what is important in our lives. If we are particularly worried about a situation at work, for example, it can make us tense, stressed or even ill. But if we can access our angel, he can calm that

stress, help us see the situation more objectively and help us cope better with the outcomes, or perhaps reveal options we could not see before. Ultimately, it is a process of slowing down and feeling for a solution, learning that we are part of a bigger picture.

When things are good, this belonging will allow you to share the joy and make it better: it can lift your spirits higher, help you find a spiritual meaning, bring you happiness. When things are okay, this contact can smooth your path, help you make decisions, bring you focus or give you renewed energy. If things are bad, you can look for comfort and solace.

Linking us with the divine

Angels can help us in bigger ways, too. One of their primary roles is to help bridge the gap between our ordinary existence and something better, between mankind and God (or your god), between this dimension and a spiritual one. The angels act as divine messengers to guide us to a better life, not in a material sense but by showing us how to be as good as possible. They show us that we are part of a wonderful universe and they are our link with the divine.

Angels sometimes do this by the example of their own actions. There are many recorded instances of a kindly stranger who offers help when someone is in distress, then disappears without waiting for any acknowledgement. This is surely a demonstration that God cares for us, as well as an experience that will only heighten our appreciation of an angelic goodness which we can try to emulate.

Sometimes angels demonstrate their divine links by precept: through the words of the scriptures of our particular religion which, over the centuries, has documented both our good and bad deeds and drawn appropriate conclusions. As the philosopher George Santayana said: 'Those who cannot remember the past are condemned to repeat it.'

Finally, angels can link us with the divine inside us – with our own better nature – by helping us to listen to the good angel on our right shoulder, to do our best and not be distracted by the sometimes easier options we could choose instead.

Angelic energy

However they manifest, angels are a force of energy. Without energy, there is simply no life. Forget running a marathon, we need energy to breathe, to see, just to exist. We need it for all our physical activity, but we also need it for our spiritual health. Why do we feel tired when we are stressed or unhappy? Why do we lose weight? It is because the heightened emotions of anxiety or sorrow sap our reserves of energy. The reverse is also true: 'I could have danced all night and still have begged for more . . .' goes the old song. Positive emotions give you an energy boost.

It follows, then, that seeking out angelic energy must be beneficial, helping to see us through bad times and making the best times truly memorable.

How can we make contact?

There are many accounts of angels appearing to people unexpectedly to offer help, hope or guidance. But you can also make yourself receptive to their energies and find ways to reach out to them.

Accidental contact

It is certainly true that many people have had experiences of angels appearing, and disappearing, out of nowhere when least expected. We may think this is completely beyond our control, and that may be so. Tradition has it that beings from another dimension need to be invited to cross the dimensional barrier – this notion is almost certainly the origin of the idea that bad spirits (notably vampires) must be invited over the threshold of your home in order to enter it. It is probable that in traumatic situations we do invoke these higher spirits by whispering a prayer asking for help and guidance; most likely it is a silent prayer from deep in our subconscious, which is where we know we really can no longer manage on our own, though we may not admit that to others or even to our own conscious, rational thought.

Angels can sense this and, as psychic beings, will use our own psychic abilities to get in touch. That little voice at the back of your mind that constantly reminds you of truths you have yet consciously to admit to yourself could be your angel oracle. The instinctive feeling you get when you just know that something or someone is going to be good (or bad) for you, when all the rational evidence points to the contrary – this could

'The guardian angels of life fly so high as to be beyond our sight, but they are always looking down upon us.'
Jean Paul Richter
(1763–1825), writer

be your angel oracle. If a series of coincidences occurs that all point towards the same decision, perhaps you should be listening. Your angel oracle is already working for you in those circumstances, but you need to be awake and alert, tuning in to what your angel is trying to tell you.

Reaching out

In those circumstances, however, our subconscious mind is already in control. In this section we look at how to make ourselves more receptive to angelic encounters by discovering techniques, including prayer, relaxation and meditation, that bring us closer to our spiritual core. By reaching that state of mind, we will be in a position to call out to the angels and make contact with them. This section examines the principles and techniques that are most useful; later in the book, various rituals and activities are described which offer ways to tailor such techniques to your particular lifestyle needs.

A healthy body

If we look after our body and health, then it it likely that we will find it easier to link into the spiritual dimension. First and foremost, this is because we will not be distracted by physical problems which limit activity. Even if we are not as young as we would like to be, or perhaps suffer from a chronic condition, it is important we try to remain as healthy and fit as we can by following a healthy diet, getting enough sleep, taking regular exercise and avoiding excesses of things that are bad for us.

It is worth choosing your favourite method of exercise carefully; if you don't select wisely, you won't continue with it. Choose something you really enjoy so that you put your heart into it – whether it is football, running, dancing or working

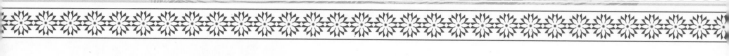

out at the gym. For many people, lower-impact exercise such as Pilates or swimming is best, while others opt for something such as yoga that offers a spiritual dimension in addition to the physical.

If you take a reasonable amount of exercise, then it's fine to indulge in the occasional double-chocolate fudge cake with cream and a glass of brandy. On the other hand, smoking and abusing drugs are definitely to be avoided. If that is a path you are treading, then hopefully your angel may be able to help you change.

The other crucial element here is that we breathe. It sounds ridiculous, because we have no choice but to breathe – it is instinctive as it keeps us alive. But thinking about our breathing and breathing deeply and fully cleanses the system and oxygenates our blood; it relaxes body and mind, brings in energy, opens up the subconscious to questions we will be asking, and increases receptivity to angelic contact.

Learning to relax

The first thing to learn is how to relax. Some people find it easy, others not so; and neither will fully understand how the other can, or cannot relax. Adapted to suit your style, it is something that everyone can learn in time. Each person has their own best way to achieve success and there is no right or wrong approach. You need to experiment, trying out different options, alternative locations and a variety of techniques, until you settle on the one that is best for you.

However far or fast you progress, the benefits of an ability to relax can be experienced in many ways, even before you make angelic contact. Our lives today are fast-paced and hectic: work is demanding, financial constraints may be an issue, relationships can be volatile. Finding a mental oasis of calm

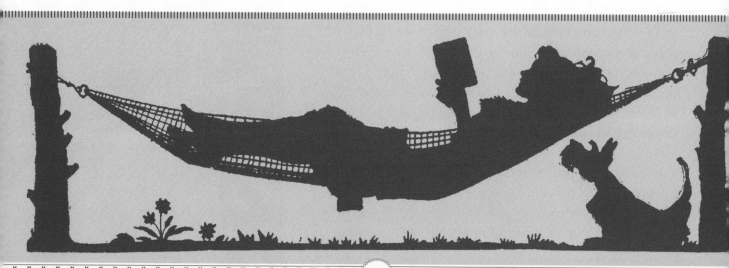

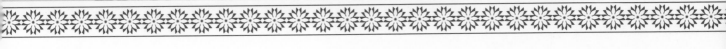

within this maelstrom can physically slow our heart rate and deep breathing increases oxygen levels. Apart from the direct physical benefits, it is important to give your mind time out; relaxing your brain stops stress from building up and helps to restore your perspective. It enables you more easily to prioritize what is most important and decide what you can and cannot realistically achieve. It also gives you the confidence to outline these targets to your boss, your friends or your family.

Furthermore, it allows you to open yourself up to a spiritual dimension: to pray to your god with total concentration. It is essential to open yourself up fully and honestly in order to lay out your concerns, your fears or your regrets to a higher power.

Making the time

If you are looking for spiritual contact you are unlikely to find it in a noisy, busy environment when your senses are already under attack on all sides and your mind is distracted by everyday thoughts: what will we have for supper tonight, how am I going to pay those bills, will I have time to finish everything in my in-tray by the end of the day?

All these pressures are too much of a distraction, so you need to make time for yourself to start on this journey. I use the word 'make' advisedly. If you wait for a spare moment, it will never come – we are all too busy and moving too fast. If an old friend telephoned to arrange a get-together, you would get out your diaries and choose a mutually convenient time. How much easier that is when there is only one diary involved – yours. Set your designated time and treat it just as seriously as you would treat a commitment to a friend. Choose a time when you can allow yourself a little while to devote to reaching out to your angel; you may only want to try five minutes or so to start with, but make sure you give full focus to the time you have. This will need to be a regular meeting, so jot down a note to yourself to remind you to relax, or later meditate, at regular intervals.

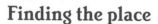

Finding the place

You need to find somewhere you feel safe and secure, where the energies are positive and where you are undisturbed. If you are fortunate you may be able to have a short while alone in your home, or perhaps you can retreat to a quiet room. Those with a busy home are unlikely to remain undisturbed so they could perhaps go to a nearby park, or even sit in the car. Solitude is important because you will be looking to separate yourself from your physical surroundings and must be able to do this without interruption. You may feel most comfortable indoors, or you may prefer to find a tranquil spot in the fresh air.

Once you have identified the place and it works for you, go back to it regularly for your angel work; this will enable you to build up powerful psychic energies on that spot.

Setting the tone

Each of us responds in different ways to different kinds of sensual stimuli – some are moved by a beautiful painting, others respond to music, and yet more to the wind on their face or a subtle fragrance.

You can use any of these stimuli to help you get in touch with your angel by creating the most conducive atmosphere to suit yourself. Use all your senses, but focus on those to which you are most responsive.

✻ **HEARING** Do you prefer silence, or perhaps some soothing music? Is there a track with particular significance, something that always makes you feel peaceful? If there is nothing specific, perhaps you could try a compilation CD of relaxing music. If you are outside, you may seek out the sound of the sea, running water or the wind in the trees.

✻ **SIGHT** Bright colours, strong sunshine or stimulating images are likely to distract you. It is usually best to dim the lights, light candles or perhaps close your eyes. Outside, dappled shade is very relaxing.

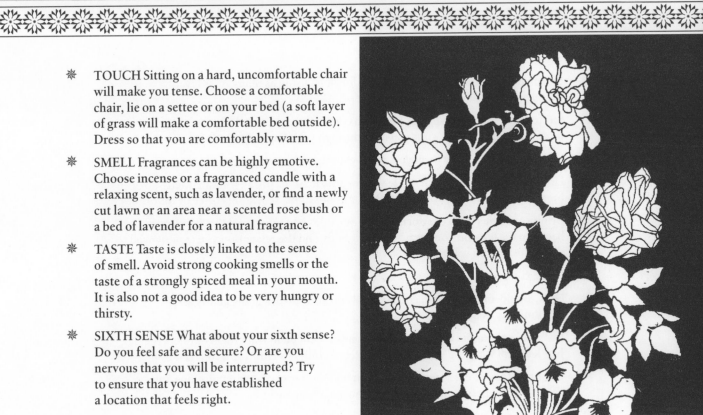

* **TOUCH** Sitting on a hard, uncomfortable chair will make you tense. Choose a comfortable chair, lie on a settee or on your bed (a soft layer of grass will make a comfortable bed outside). Dress so that you are comfortably warm.

* **SMELL** Fragrances can be highly emotive. Choose incense or a fragranced candle with a relaxing scent, such as lavender, or find a newly cut lawn or an area near a scented rose bush or a bed of lavender for a natural fragrance.

* **TASTE** Taste is closely linked to the sense of smell. Avoid strong cooking smells or the taste of a strongly spiced meal in your mouth. It is also not a good idea to be very hungry or thirsty.

* **SIXTH SENSE** What about your sixth sense? Do you feel safe and secure? Or are you nervous that you will be interrupted? Try to ensure that you have established a location that feels right.

Relaxation technique

Now you are ready to begin the relaxation process.

The first step is to try to relax completely. This should be instinctive for us, but we have lost the art and need to relearn it as a technique until it once again becomes something we can do whenever we choose, for as short or long a time as we need. Then, in stressful situations, we can take a 'step back', regain our composure, and move forward again.

Don't start by thinking about angelic contact; that will come in time. Don't think about success or failure either; those terms are too tied up in everyday stresses and are of no relevance. You may not find that you feel relaxed at first – be patient. Make short attempts, repeatedly regularly, and you will get used to the concept. As you become proficient, you will no longer need to follow the full procedure if you don't wish to; you should be able to move directly to a more relaxed state.

Some people are lucky and can simply make themselves comfortable, then relax. For these people, this section may seem tedious and they may want to skip it and move directly to the meditation section. For those who need a little more help, try the relaxation tips on the next page.

❋ Lie or sit down and make yourself comfortable, using as many or as few of the suggestions above as is appropriate.

❋ Stretch your arms above your head and concentrate on stretching every muscle and sinew from your waist up through your fingertips.

❋ Stretch your legs away from you, from your waist down to your toes.

❋ Hold that full-body stretch while you breathe in as deeply as you can, then breathe out, expelling as much of the air as possible. Repeat this three or four times.

❋ Bring your arms back comfortably to your sides and relax. Feel the difference between the tension you created in your body and the relaxation you experienced when the tension was released.

❋ Close your eyes.

❋ Now, simply breathe. Concentrate solely on your breath going gently and rhythmically in and out.

❋ Inevitably, thoughts will pop into your head. Don't entertain them or reject them. Just let them wait – as you would if it were a child interrupting a conversation.

❋ Continue for as long as you wish. If you find your everyday interruptions are becoming too persistent, end the session and try again later.

❋ Bring your awareness back to your hands and feet – wriggle your fingers and rotate your ankles and wrists once or twice.

❋ Gently roll your shoulders backwards and forwards and bring your awareness back into the room.

❋ Lie still for a few moments until you are ready to come back to everyday life.

Practise relaxing completely until you can simply use your breathing to give yourself a moment or two of respite every now and again. If you are sitting at your desk or on a bus, for example, you may want to roll back your shoulders and take a few deep breaths until you feel your body de-stressing. Enjoy the moment; recognize that it brings you a feeling of peace; allow yourself to feel that there is more to life than just getting through each day as best you can – that there is a spiritual dimension of some kind that can be uplifting.

Meditation

Meditation can perhaps be defined as relaxation taken to the next level. It is designed to help to bring you peace of mind, but also to give you a deeper understanding of your spiritual self. One of the most

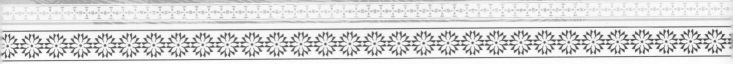

effective ways of meditating is to select something on which to focus. This could be a symbolic object, a sound, a vision of a place or a word. Some suggestions might be:

※ A feather
※ An image of an angel
※ The Buddhist 'ohm'
※ The face of someone you love
※ The word 'peace' or 'angel'
※ A candle
※ A short phrase of music

Decide what your key focus will be before you start. Follow the stages outlined above for creating the right atmosphere and for using sensual stimuli to enhance your experience. Then make yourself comfortable, go through the body stretches if you wish, and start to breathe gently but deeply.

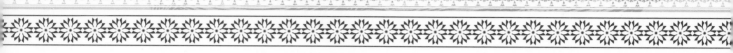

* Focus on your breathing for a few breaths.

* Now bring your key focus into your mind and, as you did before with your breathing, gently push away any thoughts that naturally spring to your mind. Feel as though you are in the middle of a pool and the mental interruptions are floating on the surface, so that as you gently touch them they simply glide away or slip beneath the surface.

* Allow everything mundane and physical to slip away from you, detach your being from your body and feel your spirit floating above your physical self, as though the two are separate.

* Enjoy the calm and the peace for as long as you feel comfortable.

* When you are ready, gradually visualize your spiritual self returning to your body and becoming one again.

* Slowly bring back your consciousness to the real world and allow yourself a little time to re-adjust before you carry on, refreshed.

Visualizing your angel

These basic techniques do not involve angels because it is easier to learn the principles before adding the angelic aspect. As soon as you feel you have become sufficiently proficient at relaxation or meditation, you can begin to introduce a further element. That is the moment to call on your angel.

The simplest way to do this is simply to visualize an angel based on an image in your mind. You can use the descriptions and images in this book, which are targeted to specific areas of spiritual energy, your own vision, a Leonardo da Vinci painting, a sculpture or something you have seen in an art gallery or a card shop. Choose something simply because you were drawn to it in some way and liked it when you first saw it.

As you breathe, focus on the image in your mind, gently pushing away other thoughts as they crop up. Don't try to wrestle with intrusive thoughts – avoid engaging with them. Remember the warm pool of water and give these thoughts a gentle nudge out of your way.

Allow the angelic image to flood your senses. You may feel an inner peace wash over you, a rush of emotion or a feeling of joy. Bask in the positive energy and absorb that energy before wishing the being farewell and promising to make contact again. Then gently return yourself to the everyday, but bring back your key image with you so that when you think of that image in future, it recalls the feelings you experienced during your visualization.

Strengthening the bond

With the description of the archangels, we included information on their correspondences, the energies associated with each angel. These can be used to make it easier to contact specific angels for particular purposes.

Using correspondences

We have already seen that different energies are interconnected throughout the universe and the spiritual realms. Using such correspondences between these energies can help you to connect with the appropriate energy, so that you can select the sensual stimuli most appropriate to the task in hand and use all the senses to get in touch with your inner angel.

The energy centres of the body, the chakras, are important in meditation:

* To energize your sense of vision, use colours, crystals or candlelight.

* To energize your sense of touch, hold a crystal, metal object or a feather.

* Your sense of smell might respond to fragrant candles or incense.

* Taste can be activated by the taste or smell of herbs.

* Your hearing can be stimulated by music, tinkling bells or sound.

Other correspondences relate to:

* The universe and astronomy: the planets, elements, lunar phases and zodiac signs.
* Time: seasons, months, days or times of the day or night.
* Numbers: the art of numerology.
* Symbols: such as halos, wings and feathers.
* Representative elements: Earth, Air, Fire and Water.

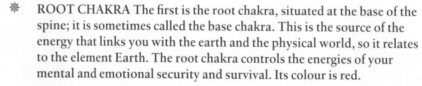

'When there is harmony between the mind, heart and resolution then nothing is impossible.'
Rig Veda (1700–1100 BC), Ancient Sanskrit collection of sacred texts

The chakras and meditation

The chakras are the seven energy centres running through the centre of the body as defined by Eastern philosophy. They absorb the energy from around you into your body and transmit your own body energy outwards, linking you with the rest of the universe. Each of the chakras vibrates to a specific type of energy.

* ROOT CHAKRA The first is the root chakra, situated at the base of the spine; it is sometimes called the base chakra. This is the source of the energy that links you with the earth and the physical world, so it relates to the element Earth. The root chakra controls the energies of your mental and emotional security and survival. Its colour is red.

* SACRAL CHAKRA The second is the sacral, or spleen, chakra in the lower abdomen. Related to emotions and therefore to the element Water, the relevant life areas are relationships, intimacy, sexuality and deep emotions, including guilt. Psychic ability is energized here. The appropriate colour is orange.

* SOLAR PLEXUS CHAKRA The third, or solar plexus, chakra is just above the navel. This is the seat of your confidence and power. Strengthening your solar plexus chakra can help you wrest back control of a situation instead of feeling out of control or even victimized. Yellow is the associated colour and Fire is its element.

* HEART CHAKRA The heart chakra, the fourth, is in the centre of the chest and is an Air energy. It deals with love, compassion and self-esteem and balances the forces of the mind and body, of yin and yang. Empathy is housed here. Green (or sometimes pink) is the colour of the heart chakra.

※ THROAT CHAKRA The fifth, the throat chakra, is at the neck. Verbal expression, communication and trust are the keynotes here, both the ability to express yourself and to understand when others are trying to communicate with you. Its colour is blue and its element is Air.

※ BROW CHAKRA The brow chakra is the sixth energy centre and it is found on the forehead between the eyes. It is sometimes called the third eye. Psychic communication resides here, with intuition and clear-sightedness. For this reason it is important to clear and energize your brow chakra to eliminate confusion and bring yourself a clearer vision. The colour associated with the brow chakra is indigo. It relates to light energy.

※ CROWN CHAKRA Finally the seventh, or crown, chakra is situated on the top of the head. Its focus is mental activity and knowledge. Difficulty in concentration may indicate that you need to stimulate the energies of this chakra. It is often associated with the colour purple.

You can use one of your chakra energy centres as a focus for meditation. Choose the chakra relevant to the priority in your life at the time. For example, if you have a problem grounding yourself and addressing an issue, you may want to meditate on the root chakra.

If your energy centres are properly balanced, you should feel physically more energized and spiritually more open. To achieve such balance, repeat your meditation technique as often as necessary, taking one chakra each time as your focus. Imagine a swirling vortex and see, in your mind's eye, the energy being sucked into the centre and emerging – a constantly flowing process. If it helps, visualize those energies cleaning out the chakra as they move through, washing away the debris that may have collected from misuse or lack of use. See that detritus cleansed from your chakra then dissolved as it is reformed and absorbed back into the ever-flowing process.

The chakras also link with specific colours and crystals so, as you become more proficient, you can layer the relationships one on top of another to create a truly firm bond.

Colours

Our response to colours is highly emotive and intuitive and the energy of colour can really help you relax, meditate and search for your angel. Colour can be used in all kinds of ways; in clothing, interior decoration, candles, lights, crystals, and so on. Of course, there are many nuances of colour, and because response to colour is very personal, you again need to be sure to make your own choice. If you feel particularly attracted to a colour, then it is likely that this the kind of energy you most need. Similarly,

if you feel uncomfortable with particular colours, they may represent something in your life that you are afraid of or trying to avoid.

- ❋ WARM COLOURS Warm colours are primarily those in the red – orange – yellow – brown range. They are energizing and stimulating both physically and emotionally, and represent the primary instincts, and therefore the first three chakras. Start with warm colours when you need stimulating, not when you are trying to calm down.

- ❋ COOL COLOURS Cool colours relate to the higher chakras and the intellectual realm. They tend to be healing, especially the green spectrum, and calming, particularly the blue spectrum. Cool colours can help you develop your intellectual abilities and reveal your strengths.

The rainbow of colours has many traditional interpretations:

- ❋ SILVER is about all that is feminine.
- ❋ WHITE is the traditional colour of purity and innocence. The energies here resonate to the highest spiritual ideals. They can be used to bring balance to all the energies you are using, to clarify the mind and emotions.
- ❋ PINK indicates romance and friendship, along with anything to do with the heart, including self-love and contentment. The colour is gentle, comforting and particularly good for children.
- ❋ RED is associated with love, as are other passions such as enthusiasm, energy and confidence.
- ❋ BROWN concerns family and responsibility; it signifies stability and connection with the Earth.
- ❋ ORANGE is all about energy, creativity and imagination.
- ❋ GOLD emphasizes the masculine principles: power, success and enjoyment of life.
- ❋ YELLOW is the colour of communication and clarity in decision-making.
- ❋ GREEN signifies security and healing, both physical and emotional. It is associated with nature, growth and natural balance.
- ❋ LIGHT BLUE brings calm.
- ❋ BLUE relates to calm and healing, the waters of life, and to meditation and dreams. It can help bring understanding and broaden your perspective.

* INDIGO suggests knowledge pursued to find wisdom. Dark blue-purple colours can help intuition and offer new ways to view a problem.

* VIOLET is a regal colour signfiying ambition and power, together with the imagination to find ways to remove obstacles.

* BLACK is grounding and stabilizing, although in some contexts it can symbolize loss or negativity. Combining warm colours with black dulls their effect without becoming too negative.

* GREY can indicate intuition or, sometimes, negative emotions. It expresses compliance and can also be used to reduce the intensity of another colour.

If you are finding it hard to make up your mind which colours are complementary to your energies, look at the two columns below, then answer the question that follows. Do it quickly and without thinking. This exercise is neither scientific nor definitive but is designed to help you find your intuitive response, rather than a response you have thought through or feel you ought to give. You have a straightforward choice between two options; simply tick the option you are most drawn to. If you start to think 'well, it depends ...' you are reading too much into it. Stop, then try again when you have only a minute to spare and cannot linger long enough to engage your conscious reasoning.

orange	blue
sunshine	showers
gold	silver
hot	warm
laugh	smile
dog	cat
dawn	twilight
diamond	opal
satin	silk
Mars	Venus
direct	subtle
red	lilac
jagged	textured
shiny	matt
spring	autumn
garnet	jade

Which column did you favour? If most of your preferences were from column 1, you need to look for colours and crystals in warm, strong colours. The more ticks you put in that column, the more likely it is

that you will respond to a richer coloured stone and a crystal form that is perfectly smooth or raw and jagged, but is unlikely to fall between the two.

If most of your preferences were from column 2, look in the cool colour spectrum – blues, dusky pinks, lilacs, greys – and at subtle tones, You may also like a smooth crystal, or perhaps one with a subtle texture rather than a rough and crystalline exterior.

Crystals

Crystals have long been regarded as receptacles of the power of the Earth, holding an energy that we can release. Colour plays a large part in how their properties are viewed, and how they relate to angelic presence. The colour values apply to crystals as to other objects, and to the chakras as outlined above, as well as to the chakra resonances. You can also decide whether you prefer a smooth, polished stone or a raw crystal. Metals can be used in a similar way.

Overlaid on to those correspondences are the intuitive responses to a colour, a texture or pattern that each individual experiences. Choose crystals for your angelic encounters that chime with the colour of your angel, the task in hand, and your own personal preferences. The table in the next few pages describes just some of the crystals you might like to use, although you will find many more available and your instinctive choice will be the right one. Think primarily about the colour and feel of the stone.

There is an infinite variety of colour variation in minerals, even in the same crystal, so this table is a guide only. Obviously you should look for a crystal of the designated colour in each group – so tourmaline, sardonyx, calcite and other stones, for example, appear more than once in the table. You will find an immense variety in crystal stores or online, so if you are drawn to another mineral, then that is the right one to choose. Let your inner angel guide you.

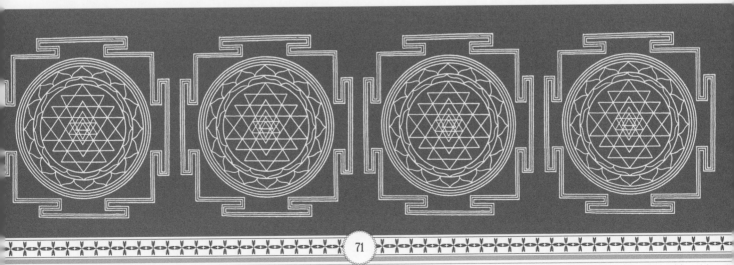

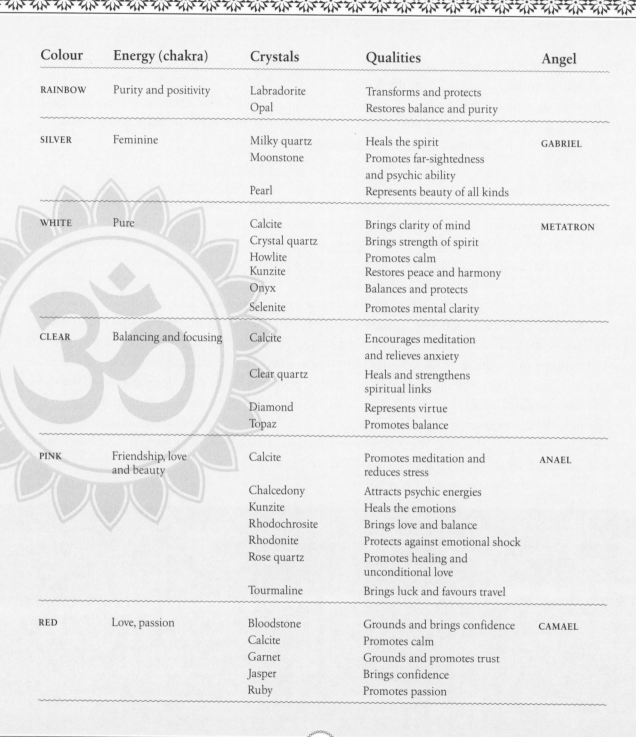

Colour	Energy (chakra)	Crystals	Qualities	Angel
RAINBOW	Purity and positivity	Labradorite	Transforms and protects	
		Opal	Restores balance and purity	
SILVER	Feminine	Milky quartz	Heals the spirit	GABRIEL
		Moonstone	Promotes far-sightedness and psychic ability	
		Pearl	Represents beauty of all kinds	
WHITE	Pure	Calcite	Brings clarity of mind	METATRON
		Crystal quartz	Brings strength of spirit	
		Howlite	Promotes calm	
		Kunzite	Restores peace and harmony	
		Onyx	Balances and protects	
		Selenite	Promotes mental clarity	
CLEAR	Balancing and focusing	Calcite	Encourages meditation and relieves anxiety	
		Clear quartz	Heals and strengthens spiritual links	
		Diamond	Represents virtue	
		Topaz	Promotes balance	
PINK	Friendship, love and beauty	Calcite	Promotes meditation and reduces stress	ANAEL
		Chalcedony	Attracts psychic energies	
		Kunzite	Heals the emotions	
		Rhodochrosite	Brings love and balance	
		Rhodonite	Protects against emotional shock	
		Rose quartz	Promotes healing and unconditional love	
		Tourmaline	Brings luck and favours travel	
RED	Love, passion	Bloodstone	Grounds and brings confidence	CAMAEL
		Calcite	Promotes calm	
		Garnet	Grounds and promotes trust	
		Jasper	Brings confidence	
		Ruby	Promotes passion	

Colour	Energy (chakra)	Crystals	Qualities	Angel
DARK RED /MAROON	Action, passion and vitality	Aventurine Jasper Sardonyx Selenite	Stimulates creativity Brings confidence Brings vitality Promotes insight	METATRON
BROWN /RED	Clear-sightedness and stability	Haematite Rutilated quartz Tiger's eye	Stimulates the mind Takes you to the heart of a problem Brings strength	URIEL
BROWN	Stability, order and the family	Amber Apache tear	Transforms negative to positive Transmutes negative to positive and brings order	
ORANGE	Energy, endurance and imagination (sacral chakra)	Calcite Carnelian Sardonyx Tiger's eye	Stimulates the imagination Encourages meditation Promotes well-being Brings strength	SANDALPHON
YELLOW	Communication and clarity (solar plexus chakra)	Citrine Fluorite Honey calcite	Brings the mind into balance and attracts prosperity Encourages communication with the spiritual dimension Brings clarity and encourages meditation	RAPHAEL
GOLD	Masculine energy, wisdom, wealth and prosperity	Gold Pyrites Topaz	Brings strength and energy Fuels positive energy and blocks negative Stimulates confidence and self-assurance	MICHAEL

Colour	Energy (chakra)	Crystals	Qualities	Angel
LIGHT GREEN	Well-being, security and calm	Amazonite	Dispels negative energy	ANAEL
		Calcite	Encourages calm and relieves stress	
		Fluorite	Encourages communication with the spiritual	
		Jasper	Nurtures	
GREEN	Healing and balance (heart chakra)	Aventurine	Heals	RAPHAEL
		Beryl	Promotes stability and relieves imbalance and stress	
		Chrysoprase	Heals	
		Emerald	Promotes recovery and wealth	
		Jade	Promotes self-reliance	
		Jasper	Nurtures and promotes spiritual development	
		Malachite	Brings humility and understanding	
		Moss agate	Promotes good fortune and well-being	
		Peridot	Reduces anger and encourages self-respect and dignity	
DARK GREEN	Unconscious knowledge and the natural world	Sardonyx	Brings forgiveness	RAZIEL
		Peridot	Calms frustration and brings self-knowledge	
		Tourmaline	Promotes spiritual communication	
LIGHT BLUE	Calm	Aquamarine	Happiness and understanding	ZADKIEL
		Blue lace agate	Heals and restores calm	
		Celestite	Encourages spiritual communication	
		Chalcedony	Attracts psychic energy	
		Howlite	Brings calm	
		Turquoise	Brings strength and confidence and protects when travelling	

Colour	Energy (chakra)	Crystals	Qualities	Angel
BLUE	Spirituality, truth and peace (throat chakra)	Angelite	Encourages communication	SACHIEL
		Aventurine	Stimulates psychic ability	
		Calcite	Relieves stress and promotes meditation	
		Celestite	Links with the spiritual dimension	
		Lapis lazuli	Heals and develops psychic abilities	
		Sapphire	Brings clarity	
		Sodalite	Encourages meditation	
		Tourmaline	Promotes spiritual growth	
INDIGO	Knowledge, intuition and meditation (brow chakra)	Azurite	Awakens psychic abilities	CASSIEL
		Iolite	Heals and encourages psychic qualities	
VIOLET	Power, psychic knowledge (crown chakra)	Amethyst	Brings peace and promotes psychic skills	SACHIEL
		Fluorite	Encourages contact with the spiritual	
		Lepidolite	Brings patience and fortitude	
		Sugilite	Heals and opens spiritual gateways	
BLACK	Grounding	Jet	Brings balance	
		Kyanite	Removes anger and restores tranquillity	
		Obsidian	Protects and grounds	
		Onyx	Balances, grounds and protects	
		Snowflake obsidian	Protects against negativity	
		Tourmaline	Protects and brings luck	
GREY	Intuitive and also softens the effect of other stones	Azurite	Develops psychic contact	RAZIEL
		Fossils	Promotes stability and sharing	
		Haematite	Stimulates the mind	
		Smoky quartz	Relieves stress and opens channels of communication	

There are many ways of using crystals and metals. For example, you can:

❋ Put a crystal under your pillow so you can absorb the positive energies while you sleep

❋ Position them around the home

❋ Wear crystal or metal jewellery

❋ Carry a crystal in your pocket or handbag

❋ Use them in rituals or prayers

❋ Carry a crystal angel or keep one in your room

Keep your crystals cleansed and active by washing them, as necessary, in clear water.

Birthstones

We all have a birthstone, and it may be that you have a particular affinity with yours. As with all these things, there are various interpretations. The most widely known modern, traditional and mystical definitions are given below.

Month	Meaning	Modern	Traditional	Mystical
JANUARY	Faith	Garnet	Garnet	Emerald
FEBRUARY	Peace	Amethyst	Amethyst	Bloodstone
MARCH	Love	Aquamarine	Bloodstone	Jade
APRIL	Virtue	Diamond	Diamond	Opal
MAY	Wealth	Emerald	Emerald	Sapphire
JUNE	Beauty	Pearl	Alexandrite	Moonstone
JULY	Passion	Ruby	Ruby	Ruby
AUGUST	Dignity	Peridot	Sardonyx	Diamond
SEPTEMBER	Clarity	Sapphire	Sapphire	Agate
OCTOBER	Purity	Opal	Tourmaline	Jasper
NOVEMBER	Hope	Topaz	Citrine	Pearl
DECEMBER	Strength	Turquoise	Zircon	Onyx

Crystals are also associated with zodiac signs and these correspondences tend to be more consistent.

❋	**Aries**	(21 March–19 April)	Bloodstone
❋	**Taurus**	(20 April–20 May)	Sapphire
❋	**Gemini**	(21 May–21 June)	Agate
❋	**Cancer**	(22 June–22 July)	Emerald
❋	**Leo**	(23 July–22 August)	Onyx
❋	**Virgo**	(23 August–22 September)	Carnelian
❋	**Libra**	(23 September–22 October)	Peridot
❋	**Scorpio**	(23 October–22 November)	Beryl
❋	**Sagittarius**	(23 November–21 December)	Topaz
❋	**Capricorn**	(22 December–20 January)	Ruby
❋	**Aquarius**	(21 January–19 February)	Garnet
❋	**Pisces**	(20 February–20 March)	Amethyst

In angelic work, you might use your birthstone or your zodiac stone to help contact your guardian angel. Birthstones can also be used to stimulate the effect of another stone.

Aromatherapy

The overlap between plants and fragrances is such that this section deals with them together. Fragrances are often used to establish a mood. It is said that smell is the most evocative and most personal of the senses.

You can use incense, oils or fragrant candles to help you in relaxation and meditation. Some fragrances help you relax, others energize you for the task in hand; you can choose your fragrances accordingly. You can also choose mixed fragrances, or combine your own. There is a huge range of essential oils available in stores and online. Some are sold as pure essential oils, but most are sold as a few drops of essential in a varying amount of carrier oil, such as almond oil, although they may still be labelled 'pure essential oil'. This will affect both the price and how you use the oil. A pure essential oil has a strong aroma; you will only need a few drops of it to create a wonderful atmosphere.

A dilute essential oil is suitable for massage or using in larger quantities. In many cases, you will need to dilute a pure essential oil.

Here are some of the uses for fragrances in your angel work.

* Scented candles bring a specific atmosphere to a room.

* Incense cones and sticks are available in various fragrances.

* Fragrant bath products can be mood-changing; use a few drops of essential oil or suitable bath product.

* Soak your feet in a bowl of warm water with a few drops of essential oil.

* Pot pourri can be used to absorb aromatherapy oils and used to fragrance a room.

* Massage oils offer an intense way of harnessing the qualities of the oil along with the tactile stimulation of massage.

* Flowers can be placed around the home for their scent and visual symbolism.

* Pots of herbs can be grown in your garden or kitchen.

* Herbal tisanes are a healthy alternative to tea and coffee.

* A few drops of essential oil on a handkerchief to be carried with you during the day.

* A few drops of essential in a bowl of hot water can be used as a cleansing inhalant.

Growing plants has added benefits as they put us in touch with the natural world and cleanse and invigorate the air around us by dispelling negativity. For this reason, you might like to keep a plant by your bedside or close to your relaxation area.

CAUTION
ESSENTIAL OILS MUST BE USED WITH CARE

Do not use essential oils on the skin unless diluted in a carrier oil.

Avoid bringing essential oils into contact with the eyes, lips and sensitive areas.

A number of oils are contra-indicated in pregnancy or after childbirth and for people suffering from specific medical conditions or taking medication.

Always follow the instructions on the product label or seek the advice of your medical practitioner.

Fragrance or plant	Qualities
AMBERGRIS	Refreshing
APPLE BLOSSOM	Enlivening
ARNICA	Stimulating
BASIL *	Warm and spicy
BENZOIN	Warming and comforting
BERGAMOT	Refreshing, soothing and uplifting
BORAGE	Cooling and soothing
CARNATION	Motivating and uplifting
CEDARWOOD *	Uplifting and reviving to encourage clear-sightedness
CHAMOMILE	Relaxing for both mind and body
CINNAMON	Energizing
CLARY SAGE *	Soothing and deeply relaxing
CYPRESS	A stimulating tonic
DILL	Good for relieving stress
EUCALYPTUS	Refreshing and stimulating
EYEBRIGHT	Astringent and stimulating
FENNEL	Toning and purifying
FRANKINCENSE	Warming and soothing
GERANIUM	Stimulating and regenerating
GINGER	Powerfully awakening and stimulating
GINSENG	Stimulating
HIBISCUS	A good tonic to enhance well-being
HONEYSUCKLE	Relaxing and cleansing
HYSSOP *	Liberating
JASMINE *	Stimulating
JUNIPER *	Astringent to sharpen the senses
LAVENDER	Soothing, calming, balancing and refreshing

Fragrance or plant	Qualities
LEMON	Refreshing and stimulating
LEMON BALM	Revitalizing and harmonizing
LILAC	Protecting
LILY	Soothing
LILY OF THE VALLEY	Brightening and enlivening
MARIGOLD	Inspiring
MARJORAM *	Restorative
MIMOSA	Relieves anxiety and oppressive memories
MINT	Refreshing and stress-relieving
MISTLETOE	Relaxing
MYRRH *	Revitalizing, cleansing and uplifting
NEROLI	Emotionally soothing and harmonizing
NUTMEG	Soothing and balancing
ORANGE	Uplifting and enlivening
PARSLEY	Cleansing
PATCHOULI	Sensual and relaxing
PENNYROYAL	Fresh and energizing
PINE	Bracing and stimulating
ROSE	Relieves stress and depression
ROSEMARY *	Enlivening to body and mind
SAGE *	Refreshing and relaxing
SANDALWOOD	Soothing and cooling
ST JOHN'S WORT	Relaxing and calming to ease anxiety
SUNFLOWER	Enlivening and inspiring
TANGERINE	Refreshing
THYME *	A tonic to alleviate anxiety
VALERIAN	Earthy and relaxing
VETIVERT	Sensuous and warming
VIOLET	Promoting change and renewal
YLANG YLANG	Soothing and relaxing

* contra-indicated in pregnancy

Your kind of music

Our response to music is so personal and the scope so broad that it is impossible to give specific recommendations for suitable music to help your angel encounters. You will know what kind of music suits your mood or helps you change it. Think about the mood you want to establish: do you want to relax, wake yourself up, try to concentrate or apply your mind to a problem? Try out different options and see which works best in different circumstances. Of course, silence may be the most appropriate.

Natural sounds are often appealing: the rush of the ocean, a tinkling stream, the wind in the trees. If you cannot experience these firsthand, search the internet for sounds available to buy on CD or to download. The sound of wind chimes or little bells can be subtle and beautiful. Wooden chimes produce a completely different sound from metal ones, and different sizes of chime give a different tone.

Music bears a close relationship to colour. In fact, some people can see colours when they hear music. Lively, upbeat music is generally associated with the warm colour spectrum – reds, oranges and yellows – while soothing music relates to greens, blues and purples.

In Buddhist temples in Thailand, visitors buy little bells to hang round the roof edges to decorate the temple. At the end of each year, sufficient precious metal has been collected to make a new statue of the Buddha; everyone has contributed and feels a part of the whole. Then, as in nature, the annual process begins again.

Phases of the Moon

The Moon has always had a huge significance for people's thinking. Perhaps the subtlety of its light has a strong connection with our intuition, our inner angel. The regularity and flow of the phases of the Moon chime in perfect harmony with the cycles of life. If you are looking for help of a specific kind, or have projects to begin or conclude, it may help to consider the phases of the Moon in relation to your timing of these things. You will find the Moon's phases in many diaries or on the internet – or simply watch the Moon for yourself and tune in to its rhythms.

* **NEW MOON** Look to the New Moon for beginnings of all kinds. It is a good time to start new projects, to plant ideas. Starting something new also means clearing away the old, so the New Moon is a great time to get out those charity bags and clean out the loft. New beginnings and growth also relate to innocence and childhood, to growth towards maturity, so this is a good time for anything to do with children.

* **WAXING MOON** When the Moon is waxing – growing to the Full Moon – then fertility and growth are the keywords. If you are developing a project, or a relationship is coming to maturity, this time will be well favoured.

* **FULL MOON** The Full Moon is when the Moon is at its most powerful. Use this power to energize any meditations or contacts. The extra energy will boost your projects.

* **WANING MOON** When the Moon is on the wane back towards the New Moon, it is a time to remove unhelpful influences, break away from bad habits and get ready for the rebirth of the New Moon.

Time

Some sources link specific angels with a season, month or even a day or an hour. For example, Raphael is said to rule the spring, Uriel the summer, Michael the autumn and Gabriel the winter. There are also different tables that link times of the day with particular angels on specific days of the week. You can find more information about this on the internet, although it would

be worth thinking first about whether you will gain any advantage by going to such lengths, especially when the correspondences are often contradictory in different sources.

On the other hand, some angels link logically with specific times of the day. The psychic, grey figure of Raziel feels comfortable in the twilight with which he is associated; the power of Michael is instinctively right at noon. Such associations can help you to time your meditation or rituals, and you will find information both in the text on individual angels and in the chapters on angel help.

The four elements

Earth, Air, Fire and Water are the four basic elements from which it was once believed everything originated. While our knowledge has since advanced more than a little, their symbolism remains strong.

- ❋ **EARTH** To evoke the energies relevant to an angel associated with the Earth, use crystals or pot plants, or surround a candle with sand. Images of spectacular mountains or other scenery can also be evocative.

- ❋ **AIR** To evoke the energies relevant to an angel associated with the Air, perhaps you could perform your ritual in the open air, or use a paper fan – or even an electric one – to circulate the air. Think about your breathing. Utilize images of the sky or clouds.

- ❋ **FIRE** To evoke the energies relevant to an angel associated with Fire, light candles or lanterns (but always be aware of safety considerations).

- ❋ **WATER** To evoke the energies relevant to an angel associated with Water, sit by a stream or use an indoor water feature. Use images of water: rivers, streams or the ocean.

Angel imagery

You can enhance your attempts to reach your inner angel by using visual images of angels or angelic symbols. Such things are all around us in everything from fine art and sculpture to amulets, embroidery, jewellery and bric-a-brac. If you find anything helpful and inspiring, then use it. Personal taste should guide you: if you appreciate the style of Pre-Raphaelite images, then a Cubist painting is not likely to help you. Cast your net wide, change your mind as often as you like, and look for all different sources. The only rules are that you are thinking positively and with a pure heart.

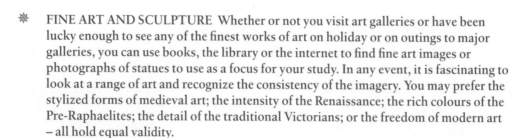

- ❋ FINE ART AND SCULPTURE Whether or not you visit art galleries or have been lucky enough to see any of the finest works of art on holiday or on outings to major galleries, you can use books, the library or the internet to find fine art images or photographs of statues to use as a focus for your study. In any event, it is fascinating to look at a range of art and recognize the consistency of the imagery. You may prefer the stylized forms of medieval art; the intensity of the Renaissance; the rich colours of the Pre-Raphaelites; the detail of the traditional Victorians; or the freedom of modern art – all hold equal validity.

- ❋ FUNERARY ART Since angels are so often represented on headstones or memorials, many beautiful images can be found in churches and other places with funerary associations.

- ❋ JEWELLERY Angel images, and particularly the flowing shape of angel wings, are often incorporated into jewellery design. A pendant or other item of jewellery makes a perfect token to keep with you to remind you that you are not alone.

- ❋ TRINKETS Little statuettes, bric-a-brac, china ornaments and so on are all available with angelic motifs.

- ❋ SYMBOLS You may prefer to focus on a simple white feather, or another symbol associated with the angel of your choice. These are listed in the text about specific angels, or in the chapters on lifestyle events.

Have I been in touch with an angel?

Manifestation can take many forms and affect just one or all of your senses. Whether you experience someone like yourself, or sense a disembodied energy, it can have a profound effect on your life.

Your experience will be unique

If you do experience an angelic encounter, the only constant is that it will be unique to you. It may be exhilarating and spiritually uplifting. Equally, it may be challenging and uncomfortable. The encounter may force you to acknowledge aspects of your personality or your actions that you would prefer not to confront. It is unlikely to provide you with instant solutions; it is much more likely to demand hard work and commitment on your part. However it manifests, if it is angelic it will be a positive and transforming experience that will make you feel loved and protected and it will put you in touch with your inner spirituality.

So how might you experience such an encounter? Angels are there to help, so they can appear in the form you are most likely to be able to assimilate, which could be through any of your senses. Encounters of all kinds have been reported and, because they are so personal, it is impossible to prove or disprove them. Someone listening objectively might believe either that angels were responsible or that the experience was simply the result of an overactive imagination. However, no amount of scepticism can invalidate the feelings of those who have found an angelic encounter positive and life affirming.

> 'The golden moments in the stream of life rush past us and we see nothing but sand; the angels come to visit us, and we only know them when they are gone.'
>
> George Eliot (1819–1880), novelist and writer

It is worth noting that while you may experience things such as a change in temperature, a touch or a sense that someone is close to you, there will never be any feeling of fear, chill or panic. The sensation will be totally natural and unforced and you will feel perfectly safe, even if you are being warned of difficulties or danger ahead. And while you may sense a warm hug or believe that someone is sitting close to you, you won't feel that such contact is inappropriate.

Consistency is another feature you can expect. You should feel that everything looks more straightforward – you might even believe you now have a step-by-step plan to resolve the issue closest to your heart – and the experience should energize and motivate you. Your inner angel will not discourage or confuse you; everything about the experience should be positive.

Miraculous intervention

There are times when angels sense your need and there are many reports of them appearing in moments of crisis, such as a car crash, and lifting people to safety or averting disaster at the last minute, only to disappear from the scene and prove totally untraceable. In these cases, they may appear as humans or in angelic form.

Angels may appear to people when they are at their lowest ebb and feel they can't go on. Sensing that people are in great need is part of the angels' protective nature and some reports claim that angels have even intervened to prevent people from taking their own life.

Earth angels — the helpful stranger

Another commonly described occurrence is when a helpful stranger appears from nowhere to assist you out of a difficult predicament. Once his job is done, the angel disappears, leaving no clue as to his identity, although to all intents and purposes he seemed like an ordinary person.

In former times, it might have been possible for someone to offer a helping hand to a stranger in need, then quietly slip away unnoticed and remain unknown and undiscovered. Nowadays, however, with CCTV cameras and social networking websites, it is hard to understand how anyone could completely disappear in such a way.

British TV presenter Gloria Hunniford is a believer in angels. She relates how, while driving in heavy traffic with her husband through France, she momentarily lost concentration and found herself tearing

across the road between articulated trucks and crashing against a concrete pillar. All their belongings were strewn across the road and, while her first thought was to call an ambulance as her husband was bleeding, she could not help worrying about what was going to happen to their possessions. At that point, a beautiful young girl with long blonde hair emerged from the crowd and asked: 'Would you like me to look after your things?'. Agreeing without hesitation, Gloria met up with the girl again the next morning. The girl took Gloria and her husband to the local garage to pick up the car and their belongings. After that morning, the girl was never seen again and no one in the town had seen or heard of her, or knew anything about her.

A new person in your life

At some moments in our lives, we meet a new person whose influence is so profound it can be life-changing. On a TV show, Joey Daniels explained how he found himself in prison, angry and full of self-loathing but with no idea of who to turn to or how to make the changes he knew he should make to his lifestyle and behaviour. Then he met Mick, who talked to him about God and challenged his views of life and the inevitability of the path he was taking. Joey believes Mick was the angel sent to stop him from going down the road to self-destruction. His change of attitude was so dramatic that he could only attribute it to angelic intervention.

It is worth noting that we cannot predict how changes will be made and it may not necessarily be just coincidence when someone comes into our lives at a particular time.

Feathers and rainbows

These are traditional symbols of the presence of angels, so if you see an incongruous white feather, watch it and think about its significance. TV presenter Gloria Hunniford's daughter Caron Keating, also a presenter, died from breast cancer in 2004. Gloria regularly comes across single white feathers in unexpected places, which she believes are messages from her daughter in heaven. It began on the day of Caron's funeral when a feather fell at Gloria's feet. She said: 'It's extraordinary because I am constantly finding isolated feathers, including one in the studio today

– even though there were no feathers around. I find it a great comfort.'

Other people have reported seeing angels in the clouds or reflections on still waters, a beam of protective light shining along a path to guide the way, or a rainbow appearing when there is no sunshine and no showers.

Detection of the aura of someone you meet can also indicate that this person is special to you. The aura is an electromagnetic field that surrounds each of us; it is a demonstration of soul energy and therefore reflects, in an oval rainbow of coloured light, a person's spiritual nature. The aura is divided into layers: astral, emotional, mental and spiritual. Most people have an 'imperfect' aura, reflecting their human nature, so the colours vary with their character and mood. Happiness engenders a bright, dancing aura in warm colours, whereas sadness darkens and dulls the aura and slows down the movement. An angel has a perfect aura – a halo of light surrounding him – of a pure colour associated with his energy.

Repeating patterns

In the film *The Matrix*, a repeating pattern – déjà vu – signals a disturbance in the matrix of life. In our lives, a repeating pattern may indicate that our subconscious angel is trying to attract our attention. Perhaps a number, colour or symbol keeps cropping up. It may be that a name appears repeatedly – it could be the name of your angel. Pay attention, think about the associations and see if you can ascertain to what it relates.

It is said that if an angel is trying to help you but you are ignoring the signs, the angel will persevere and keep repeating the symbol or gesture in different ways. Therefore you need to think whether a repeating pattern in your life is a coincidence after all. Don't give up: keep asking questions until you understand the message you are being given. Your inner angel oracle will find the answer in the end, so trust your intuition and think from your subconscious if you have a problem that does not stand up to logical thought. This is equally true whether you believe in angels as external beings or if you are focused on your intuitive inner angel.

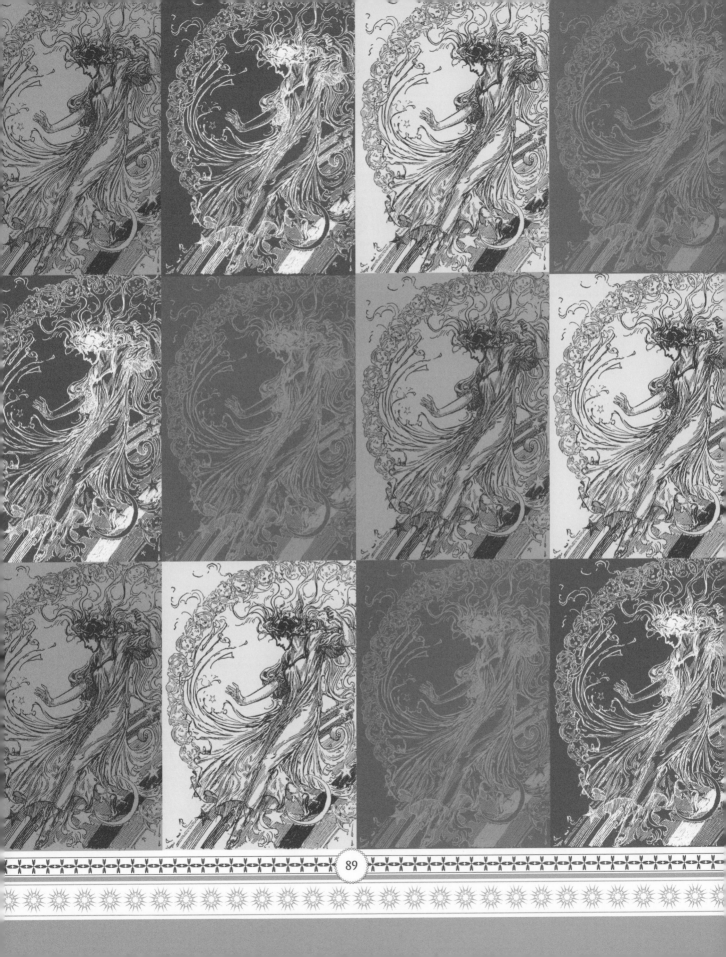

Music and laughter

It may be that you hear rather than see an angel. If your hearing is finely tuned, this may be the way the angels choose to contact you. Soft laughter, tinkling bells and unexplained strains of beautiful music on the wind could all indicate the presence of an angel. Other reminders that angels could be near might be hearing the doorbell ring when there is no one there, or hearing something on the TV or radio that is relevant to a question you have been asking, or overhearing a conversation that gives you the clue you need to solve a problem. Music is likely to be something you, personally, find beautiful and it will never be discordant.

You may hear a voice and, if so, it will be one that is reassuring and gives clear advice; it will never be abusive, threatening, harsh or unkind. There may be circumstances in which the best advice involves changes that need to be made in your life, in practical or emotional terms, but you will feel that the suggestion is given kindly, with your best interests at heart. Quite possibly, the voice may sound familiar, although you will probably not be able to place it; many people say that they know it is not their own voice, but sometimes has some characteristics of their voice within it.

A comforting touch, a waft of fragrance

The physicality of human touch is immensely comforting. It is even more reassuring to be embraced by an angel. Some people have reported such experiences, as well as sensory experiences such as smelling sweet flowers. This resulted in a wonderful feeling of calm.

It is important to reiterate here that any apparent physical contact – be it an embrace or the feeling of being

very close to someone – will always be protective, comforting and appropriate and will never have sexual overtones.

Animals also react to changing energy patterns – for example, dogs and horses can grow skittish on windy days – and a cat may begin to purr for no apparent reason in the presence of an angel.

A surge of energy

An encounter with an angel can also be experienced beyond the senses: as an overwhelming feeling of euphoria, peace or joyous anticipation, a sudden burst of laughter or feeling of inspiration. The feeling might be unexpected and apparently unrelated to the specific circumstances. Alternatively, you may have been meditating or studying your angel and might really feel you have made contact. It is often the case that such feelings are experienced in conjunction with other sensory angelic contact.

What if I don't make contact?

There are a number of factors that can prevent angelic contact, or getting in touch with your inner angel, but foremost among them is negative energy. Angels are pure positive energy. Just as the poles of two magnets can either attract or repel, negative energy can drive away the positive energy trying to reach you. You need to be open to new influences, feel positive and be sensible in your expectations.

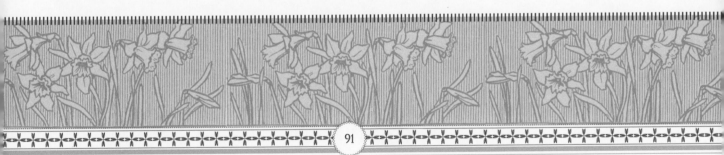

If the intensity of trauma in your life is responsible for negative energy, then it makes the situation difficult to combat. The first thing to do is to try to conserve enough strength to pray for help and support. Just for the time being, think only of today. Try the relaxation exercises to gain some rest and, hopefully, sleep. That will help to restore your inner balance and give you the energy to move on a step at a time, keeping yourself open to help from all quarters. Do not refuse help from a friend or neighbour – it may be that the angels sent them to you.

Unrealistic expectations are a hindrance to linking with your inner oracle. Do not fall into the trap of believing that there are instant miracles around every corner; the angel oracle can only show you how to perform miracles for yourself.

Impatience is another barrier to communication. Although spiritual energies are supportive, they are not simply at our beck and call. Step back a pace and, again, practise the relaxation techniques to restore your sense of balance.

The angel within

One concern raised by sceptics about people who believe in angels is that if times are difficult and their angel does not 'appear' to sort things out, the sense of abandonment can be devastating. However, if you believe that angelic energy is fed into your own personal strength to help you solve your problems, then this argument no longer applies.

Finding Yourself

Whether you define your goal as happiness, contentment or spirituality, these things can only be brought about by your own intense efforts. Those who sit and wait for a miracle to happen will be waiting a long time.

Look around you — who is making waves? The chances are it will be the people who grasp opportunities, who find some inner confidence and take action. They will not always be those who act selflessly — in fact, it is likely that good proportion of these movers and shakers will be looking primarily to their own advantage — but this need not detract from the lesson that bold, positive action is rewarded. There are plenty of examples of good people who make a real difference — Mother Teresa, Bob Geldof, Bill Gates, Nelson Mandela — and these should be our role models.

What they all possess is an inner confidence. Some people may be born with it, but for many of us it is not so easy to find. However, every journey begins with a first step, as the Chinese proverb says. In this section we look at the practical steps you need to take to set off on your journey of spiritual discovery, which will ensure that you reach your destination safely.

Establish your starting point

Regard the process of finding your inner angel as a journey you know you must embark on without knowing quite where you will end up. The general direction is clear but the specifics will need to be worked out on route. You may change path along the way, stop to rest, slow down or speed up, or get half way and take a different route altogether. The first thing to recognize is that knowing where to start is even more important than knowing where you are going. Mark your place on your map first, then you can start to track your progress towards your destination.

You can make it happen

Standing still and waiting achieves nothing in the long run, but stopping to assess and reflect is an important way of helping you to define where you need to take action, what your priorities are and which aspects of your life should be tackled first. You will be very fortunate if there is only one thing in your life you would like to change, but if you go full speed ahead trying to alter everything at once, you are less likely to succeed.

Use this time of reflection to make an inventory of your life to galvanize your spirit to take you forward.

'Learn from yesterday. Live for today. Hope for tomorrow.'
Albert Einstein
(1879–1955),
physicist

Where am I and where am I going?

Some people may find themselves at a crossroads, wanting to make changes or unsure of their direction. For those people, looking at where your life's path has taken you can help you to see clearly the good things you have achieved.

Time for an appraisal

A review of your life needs to have a purpose. Going over old ground can be wearying and unproductive, so start with a clean sheet of paper – or a new document – and write your name at the top of it. Now write a reminder to yourself: I am looking back only so that I can look forward.

Take a good look at yourself and where you are in your life. Write down some ideas. You may find that things come out in a jumble and you end up scribbling in all directions on your paper. That doesn't matter. If you wish, you can tidy the information into neat columns under appropriate headings (but only if you find that helpful). Your ideas might include:

❋ Family: the people you are closest to and can rely on

❋ Friends and colleagues

❋ Relationships: partners

* **Talents:** your best qualities
* **Education:** achievements
* **Qualifications:** craft skills
* **Work situation:** employment status
* **Health:** current situation

'Our greatest glory is not in never falling, but in rising every time we fall.'
Confucius (551–479BC), philosopher

In each case, list the good things first. Accentuate the positive, even if it seems like a small detail. Then think about those things you would like to change. Be realistic about your shortcomings, but don't dwell on them. For every weakness, think of a way you could turn it into an advantage – look for the silver lining behind the cloud. Remember to look for the good in yourself. Leave some space for what to do next.

You might have filled your page or you might be baffled as to what to write. If the former, you won't need much help. But if you are not sure what to put, there is an example of what your appraisal might look like on the next page. Ignore the 'what to do' heading for the time being – we'll come to that later. Your appraisal doesn't need to be an essay, or even make sense to anyone but you. It is simply a device to help you organize your thoughts.

FAMILY

GOOD	• Mum
BAD	• Brother Pete
	• Fell out with Pete over boyfriend Mike borrowing money
SILVER LINING	• Not seeing Mike any more
WHAT TO DO	• Help Mum in the house a bit more
	• Ring Pete and buy him a drink to say sorry

FRIENDS

GOOD	• Mary and Jim – neighbours
	• The girls from school
BAD	• Not much in common with most of the people at work
SILVER LINING	• Sally from work is fun
WHAT TO DO	• Organize a trip to the cinema with Sally – get out more!

TALENTS

GOOD	• I like clothes and I'm smart
BAD	• Mum says I am too talkative
	• Disorganized
	• I like shopping too much
SILVER LINING	• People like me the way I am
WHAT TO DO	• Sort out the wardrobe and do a charity bag
	• Talk to Mum about budgets (maybe)

EDUCATION

GOOD	• 4 GCSEs
BAD	• Couldn't leave school soon enough

QUALIFICATIONS

BAD	• You're joking!
WHAT TO DO	•Look at evening classes or something – no idea what

RELATIONSHIPS

BAD	• Not since Mike dumped me
SILVER LINING	• It was never going to work
WHAT TO DO	• I'm not bothered at the moment

WORK SITUATION

GOOD	• Job in the supermarket – at least it's a job!
BAD	• Boring – no future
SILVER LINING	• At least I'm getting paid
WHAT TO DO	• Stick with it and keep an eye out for something better

HEALTH

GOOD	•Yeah, good
	• Nothing bad here – hurrah!
	• Nothing to stop me

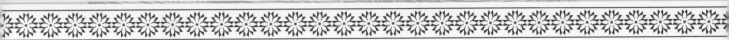

This is quite enough for a start because it shows you where you are on your map, and the vehicle and fuel you must marshal to take you where you want to go. It's not a Porsche? Join the club! There's no point pretending to yourself that 'this time next year, you'll be a millionaire'; we have to work with what we have. Your means of transport may be a reliable family car with plenty of people on board, a clapped out old banger or just you in a pair of down-at-heel trainers. The angels don't care as long as what you seek is to make life better and reach out to the part of yourself that is on a higher plane.

A little time travel

Now you need to decide which direction you are going in, so look at the headings you wrote down earlier and fill the space you left at the bottom for what to do. Use pencil to emphasize that it's not written in stone (if you are using a computer, you can change it easily anyway). If you look back at the example, you'll see it offers a few specifics to start with – so you can do the easy things first, then look at the more demanding options and think some more.

Finally, you may want to consider where you would like to be in a year's time; if that's too much for your current circumstances, then don't write it until you are ready. Your answer may just be: I want to be anywhere but here! That's as good a start as any. Remember to be realistic; saying you'd like to be that millionaire driving a Porsche might be fun for a daydream but it is better to start with more modest ambitions. If you have a goal in mind, start to think about what you need to do to make it a reality. Goals will inspire us if they are achievable with hard work and application.

What has this to do with angels?

It might appear that we've lost the angelic thread completely, but remember the importance of the angel oracle – that intuitive inner gift. Knowing yourself, looking at your character and your actions clearly and honestly and without excuses – as you may believe God will look at them in the final reckoning – is crucial for developing a relationship with your innermost angel oracle. Only by really knowing yourself will you be able to make that contact with a higher spirituality. If you are in touch with your inner angel, that may be all the guidance you need; or it may be a stepping-stone to contact with the angels.

Take control

Angelic help can invigorate and support you, but is not a miracle cure. If you take practical steps to help yourself, you will find that spiritual support can become more meaningful.

Help me to help myself

Now that you have made an assessment of your situation, you need to think about what you want to do to make changes for the better. You can begin your search for greater spirituality, but you should also muster the strength and confidence to take some practical steps to make things happen in your life. Remember this is a step-by-step process so you may need to address some practical issues before you embark on more spiritual ones. If practical issues persistently come top of your priority list, your intuition is trying to tell you something, so listen to it.

If you have not already started on a programme of relaxation, meditation or prayer, then now is the time. Whatever you feel is right for you is the right thing to do and will have benefits. Take your time and try not to focus on end results during this activity. It could take time, practice and patience to get in touch with your intuition, but follow the instructions, adapting them to your character and beliefs, and you will make progress.

Look at the list you made in the previous exercise and highlight the improvements you felt you needed to make. Number them in order of priority, then focus on number one. It is far better to work on one thing at a time because it allows you to put all your energy, both spiritual and physical, into one thing, and gives you a greater chance of success.

Take a sheet of paper and write your chosen objective in the middle. It could relate directly to looking for more spirituality in your life or it could be as prosaic as 'Lose weight', 'Work

'You have an opportunity to be in control of your life for yourself by the decisions that you make.'
Sean Combs (Puff Daddy) (b. 1969), musician

harder at school', 'Do more exercise'. Give yourself a specific target and write that down underneath. If your intentions are too vague, you'll never make them a reality. Now play a word association game and jot down ideas on your paper – anything you can think of that will help you achieve your goal. Look at the list of ideas below for examples of things to include.

'It's the friends you can call up at 4 a.m. that matter.'
Marlene Dietrich (1901–1992), actor

Role models and friends

It helps to look at how other people make a success of their lives. If you choose your role models carefully, they can be a real inspiration. Think about the people you admire – it could be anyone from your mum to Barack Obama. What is it about them that you particularly respect? Think about whether there are characteristics you could emulate to your advantage. It is not always the 'big' things that matter the most. Obama may have huge power and influence but, to those close to him, it may be his thoughtfulness in little things that is more important.

Be careful not to think that everything about your role model is perfect, however. This will only result in you believing, mistakenly, that you pale into insignificance beside them, especially if they are famous and you don't actually know them. If you do feel yourself falling into that trap, there is a simple solution. Imagine a scenario in which they look totally ridiculous or utterly mundane: Obama as a pantomime dame, your favourite film star falling over in a muddy field, a world-famous political leader cleaning his teeth. Just bring that image to mind and it will bring them down to size. Whether or not they are your role models, don't cut yourself off from family and friends who may be able to help you. Few people are strong enough to achieve things alone. Look outwards not inwards and enlist the help of those around you.

IDEAS
- People who will help
- Places to go for support
- Things you would like to achieve
- Problems you might encounter
- Questions you need to answer
- Tasks to do
- Jobs you really don't want to do but feel you should
- Contacts
- Priorities
- Role models – whose actions you could copy
- Negative role models – the people not to look to as examples

Small, steady steps

It is no good wanting to go to the Moon if you only have a rusty bicycle. Go back to your plan and see how realistic it is. Following our example, did you say you'd run three miles every day for the first week, then four miles after that? A target should be an ambition that encourages you to do your best, not an improbable goal that ensures you'll fall at the first hurdle.

You have already numbered your list, so stick with that. Focus on number one, then gradually move on, adding other tasks to your 'to do' list.

Another old proverb reminds us that habits are harder to break than principles. You may want to go for a walk every morning – that's a good intention but it's something you have to think about and work at. You have been cleaning your teeth each morning and putting on your seat belt every time you get in the car for so long that you wouldn't think of not doing these things. They are habits – good ones. So bring your new activity of going for a walk each day up to the level of habit. Make it fit into your existing routine and, very soon, it will just be second nature.

Visualization

Imagining good outcomes – daydreaming, if you like – is always good, but visualization is taking it a step further. It is not so difficult to imagine good things happening to you, but visualization is more than that – it is about living the dream in your mind's eye. But, just like a fantasy film, it is vital that it is internally consistent and follows its own logic. When you are visualizing the achievement of your goals, you will be immersed in the experience, taking yourself once again on to that spiritual plane.

Decide on the subject of your visualization, keeping it as simple as you can. Relate it to what you most want to achieve and try not to be distracted by other issues. If it helps, break down your visualization into component 'scenes'. For this example, let's say you want to apply for a new job but are lacking the confidence to take the first step. Follow the procedures on pages 58–61 to find a suitable place and time, and to make yourself comfortable.

❋ Again, use these familiar techniques to relax and take yourself out of your physical self.

* Now bring yourself into your mind's eye as though you were a fly on the wall. Ask yourself: 'What's the worst that can happen if I apply for the job?' Visualize yourself with a swift answer: 'I don't get the job – so I'll apply for something else.' Really *feel* your response: it may not be what you want, but you can certainly cope with it.

* Experience the feeling of getting up out of your chair and going to the computer. Feel how confidently you are walking – standing straight and smiling.

* In your mind's eye, log on to the website and open the application form. Fill it in onscreen, print it off and check it through. Actually feel the experience of completing the application and logging off.

* Now bring yourself back to the real world, bringing that confidence with you.

The first time you try visualization, it may be difficult – you may not be able to imagine yourself acting in a more confident way – but practice will bring improvement. You can repeat the process as often as you need, and each time you should feel more empathy with the confidence and resolve of your alter ego. If you really cannot see yourself in your visualization, try watching someone you admire and copying their behaviour.

'Believe you can and you're halfway there.'
Theodore Roosevelt (1858–1919), US president

Sometimes your subconscious may throw up problems. In the visualization, the website might crash or an error message may appear. Don't give up! Visualize solving the problem: restart the computer, search the help pages, resubmit the form. Do it calmly and with a smile. Your subconscious might try to trick you into abandoning the project: a flower might grow out of the screen, or the wireless mouse may scuttle away. Remain calm and dismiss this unconscious sabotage. Each time you persevere, your resolve will strengthen until you feel ready to do it for real. Then you can move on to the next phase.

You may like to introduce some angelic support into your visualization. Choose an angel to stand behind your shoulder to encourage and support you. If you prefer, think about how this exercise is strengthening your inner angel, allowing you to get in touch with what really matters to you.

Positive affirmation

Another technique you can use to awaken your inner angel is positive affirmation. Put simply, you repeat a phrase so often and with such conviction that it becomes a belief.

Choose a short phrase, but one that is apposite and inspirational. 'I will take more exercise' is a bit vague. 'I will walk to the paper shop every morning this week' or 'I will pray for five minutes before I go to sleep' are more useful.

Repeat your mantra ten times before breakfast and ten times before you go to sleep. Throughout the day, keep reminding yourself of its positive message.

- ❉ Repeat it to yourself
- ❉ Put a Post-it note on the fridge
- ❉ Put a sticker on your car keys
- ❉ Write it in your diary
- ❉ Make a notice for your desktop
- ❉ Slip notes inside drawers so that you come across them when you are looking for your socks

It is such a simple process that you may think it cannot be successful, but it is possible gradually to change your attitude by constant reaffirmation of sound principles.

Keep a journal

Many people find that writing things down is a great help when dealing with problems, so get a notebook, your diary, smart phone or anything else in which you make notes, and start a clean sheet. Jot down the date and the nature of the issue you are trying to solve, then each time you make progress, encounter a problem or have an idea, jot down your feelings. You may just like to use it to get something off your chest. Writing down your hopes and dreams, or your frustrations, can put them into perspective and be a safety valve, too, to vent anger or disappointment harmlessly.

You may go back over your notes or, more likely perhaps, never look at them again. It really doesn't matter. Just as you may remember your shopping list without referring to it once you have written it down, there is something about the process of putting words on paper (literally or virtually) that is immensely powerful.

Again – what does this have to do with angels?

There is a double advantage here. On the one hand, using these techniques will already have brought you much more in touch with your inner angel – with what you know is right for you. Taking action to deal with practical issues will hopefully result in an improvement to your everyday circumstances. The resolution or diminishing of problems will reduce their impact and give you more time and energy to think about spiritual issues and to make further changes in your life. By clearing your mind of some of your problems you should find it easier to work on your relaxation technique and make yourself even more receptive to contact with your angel oracle. Remember, the objective is to tap into spiritual energy to bolster your reserves and resources, not to replace them. You are still the person making things happen. Don't forget to keep congratulating yourself on your achievements.

Angels in Your Life

Throughout our lives there are milestones we want to remember and low points we would rather forget. The only thing that is certain is change — which could be for good or bad — but is simply a part of life.

Wherever you are in the roller-coaster of existence, for every circumstance, each trial and tribulation, you can find strength to help you through angelic contact.

In this section, we consider specific times in your life when you need help and guidance or want to express exhilaration and joy, and will look at ways in which you can find angelic energy to intensify those good feelings and soften the negatives. There are first-hand accounts of people's experiences to inspire you to find your angel oracle.

The purpose of seeking this contact is to help you seek out the goodness inside yourself, to understand yourself better and enable you to lead a happier life in tune with your highest values, and those of the world, the people around you and the divine principle.

An angel for every day

We have already looked at the choirs of angels and identified that they all have different characteristics and can help us in different ways. When it comes to making contact, it makes sense to focus your attention on the energy that is most suited to alleviating your problem. The best way to do that is

to focus on one of those angels. If you needed a new light fitting, you would not call a plumber. A gardener might be more than willing to help you paint your house, but you would be better off asking a decorator. In each of the following chapters, which focus on various life experiences, we will suggest the most appropriate angelic energy to tap into. Although we have associated each energy with a particular archangel, there are more angels than we can reasonably be expected to count, so your response may come from within, or from any number of angels who are waiting to guide and support you.

Ask your angel oracle

All through life, we encounter ups and downs, problems and challenges. To help yourself stay on track, set aside a little regular time – it could be two minutes, it could be an hour or more – to speak with your inner angel.

There are many words people use to describe what you are aiming to achieve. We might say you are communing with your angel oracle; others may describe it as accessing your deepest intuition, discovering what's in your heart or defining your gut reaction to an issue. The fact is that you do know, deep in your subconscious, what is best for you and one way of finding out that information is to access the positive energy of the angels through your subconscious mind.

You may not find it easy in the beginning but, with practice, it will become second nature. You may not believe, or be able to accept, any messages you receive at first. Be patient and wait. You do not have to act straight away – it may not be the right time for you; let the thoughts rest in your mind until you are ready.

You may find that performing the relaxation technique (see pages 61–62) in full is best, or you might like to try the abbreviated version of this exercise on the next page.

> 'I saw the angel in the marble and carved until I set him free.'
> Michelangelo Buonarroti (1475–1564), artist

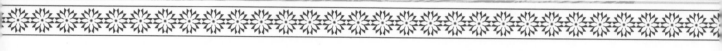

- ❋ You need a quiet place, unless you are skilled at blocking out everything else.

- ❋ Make sure you are sitting comfortably so you are not distracted by physical interference.

- ❋ Close your eyes, if you like, and take a few deep breaths; relax your body.

- ❋ Focus on the angel you have chosen and allow the issue in question to rest in your mind, but try not to think actively about it.

- ❋ What does your angel say? What is your gut reaction? What is the first thing that comes into your head?

- ❋ Follow that line of thought and see where it leads you.

- ❋ As soon as you feel you have an answer, or a direction to follow, gently bring yourself back to the real world, take a few more deep breaths and stretch out your body.

- ❋ The time may be right to act on your angelic message or it may not; only you can decide what to do next.

The time must be right

Even if you know what is right for you, that is not the same as being in a position to realize your dream or take whatever action is needed to set a process in motion. There is 'a time to every purpose under heaven,' it says in Ecclesiastes (3:1), and it is a good thing to remember. Take your time to ponder on the advice given by your angel oracle; you will know when the time is right to act.

Feel the Force

Anyone familiar with the *Star Wars* films will recognize the process of accessing your inner angel oracle in this way: you need to feel the Force. In these movies, the Life Force pervades the universe and, with study and practice, can be accessed by those who need it. The essence of the process is to stop thinking, give up conscious control and trust your instincts.

Angels to help you focus

For those new to thinking about angels, or about spiritual matters in general, a gentle introduction can be the best option. A sensitive angel is the best one to help you understand more about how to move forward.

Finding an angel to sharpen your focus

When you don't know where to start, or how to make a decision, when you know that change is needed but have no idea how to go about making it happen, an influx of energy to help you focus on the issues at hand can be immensely supportive.

Deep in your subconscious, you may know what needs to be done, and now you should be beginning to understand the process of turning to your angel oracle in order to access that inner wisdom.

In these circumstances, you need the energy to stop, look and listen, to make an assessment of what

> 'One reason so few of us achieve what we truly want is that we never direct our focus; we never concentrate our power. Most people dabble their way through life, never deciding to master anything in particular.'
>
> Anthony Robbins (b. 1960),
> writer

is the best thing to do, so you specifically require clear-sightedness, knowledge and access to unconscious wisdom. The angel we will use to help you focus is Raziel, although if you prefer to think about your guardian angels or already have knowledge of another angel who could help you, then you can call to them instead.

Raziel possesses the deep, unconscious wisdom we are seeking, so he can help to energize our inner oracle, where we can understand our most fundamental needs. He reassures us that it is sound to trust our instincts and psychic abilities and this gives us confidence. With access to his clear-sightedness, we can achieve a better perspective and see what is really important to us. Concentrating on Raziel's energies can facilitate contact with our inner angel oracle so that we can start the process of spiritual growth.

Raziel meditation

Thinking about Raziel involves making contact with your intuition. If you have been practising relaxation and meditation, this exercise will bring together the work you have already done; if you are only beginning to implement the exercises, this is the perfect incentive to put the ideas into practice.

You will need to gather any correspondences you choose to use for this meditation. Think about what might help you. You could burn some uplifting cedarwood incense, or perhaps opt for ginger or cypress; if you feel you need something more calming than stimulating, lavender or chamomile might be good. If you wish to hold a crystal, choose dark green to stimulate your unconscious knowledge – perhaps peridot or green sardonyx – or grey to encourage your innate intuition – a smoky quartz or fossil. You can also combine a grey stone with one of a stronger colour to soften its influence. If you can meditate outdoors, that will highlight Raziel's associations with the element Air.

Think about when would be a good time for your meditation. With his focus on subtle psychic energies, Raziel is linked with twilight, so that might be an appropriate time to try this exercise, as the light is softening and fading and objects in the physical world become less distinct, allowing you to focus on spiritual things.

* Find a suitable place for meditation, somewhere you can be comfortable and remain undisturbed, where the light is soft and dim.

* Light your candles or incense, if you are using them, and have your crystals with you.

* Settle yourself comfortably and breathe in the fragrance, taking long, deep breaths. Close your eyes. Concentrate fully on your own gentle, rhythmical breathing.

* When you are ready, visualize yourself sitting alone in a beautiful place. It could be a garden, on a hillside, in a palace or a garden shed, on a tropical beach or in a comfortable room of your own home. You feel comfortable there. Fill it with things that make you feel secure in yourself, or leave it empty if that feels right.

* Now visualize a green ball of light coming slowly towards you, gradually increasing in size until, when it reaches you, it envelops you in a sphere of light. Feel totally calm and comfortable; bathe in the light as long as you wish.

* As the energies swirl around you, see the angel Raziel within them, bringing you the gift of his energy.

* Gradually feel the aura of light reducing in size, with its centre at your brow chakra. Feel the energy becoming more intense as it does so, and imagine that you are absorbing those spiritual energies.

* What you sense next will be unique. You may simply feel calm and relaxed, you may feel energized or you may experience inner peace or joyous emotion. Enjoy it.

* Encapsulate the spiritual energy you have experienced in an image of Raziel and watch as you absorb that energy into yourself.

* As the light fades, gradually concentrate again on your breathing to bring yourself back to the everyday. Hold on to that image of Raziel in your mind so that his energy is absorbed into your own.

Learning to relax

Learning to relax completely is a hugely valuable skill to develop, and it increases in importance with the pace of your life. Both physically and mentally, we ignore the value of switching off at our peril. If you practise relaxation techniques regularly, there will come a point when you are able to 'power down' at will and recharge your batteries for a few short moments when you most need the boost.

Using the energy

The best outcome is that the surge of energy has put you in touch with your angel oracle. If so, then – almost without thinking about it – you will know what you now have to focus on in your life. Priorities and decisions will become easier

Your own experience may be slightly different but should certainly include a feeling that you are calmer and have a more balanced view of your situation. With that clearer energy, go back to your life plan or your questions and ask them again. Use the renewed energy and clearer focus to shine that light on your situation and help you identify what is most important to you, so that you can then take steps to move your life forward.

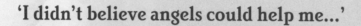

'I didn't believe angels could help me…'

'There are times when I have wished that I shared the absolute trust in angels, especially guardian angels, that some people have.

'One such time I was sitting on the hard shoulder of the motorway waiting for the breakdown truck because my clutch had given out in the middle lane and I had to push and freewheel the car across to the side. I was supposed to be going to the seaside with an old friend and had been looking forward to it for weeks. The new clutch the car needed was going to cost me £600 on top of what seemed like the most expensive week of my life. The back door of the house had finally seized up and the new one was on order – £850. The loo decided it needed replacing – £700 – plus I had no idea what the plumber would charge for the further work I was advised I needed. The roof repairs added £650. I was worried about my daughter and two of my nieces who were living in an unsafe district of London. Plus I'd been made redundant a few months before, so I was only just getting used to my new, and reduced, financial arrangements. Oh, and I had just wiped out my savings by paying for my holiday (so that bit was not all bad!).

'I didn't dare ask what else could go wrong. Wouldn't it be perfect if some kindly stranger pulled up and said, 'Oh, it's not the clutch, it's just this loose wire – there you are, all sorted', then drove off. At least that would be one problem solved.

'But then I realized what a ridiculous idea that was. Life doesn't work like that, does it? If no one had to try, to make an effort, to work, to do anything but wait around for an angel to sort things out, everything would just grind to a halt!

'We all need our inner angel just as I do: to maintain focus, to put us in touch with everything that is good – and keep reminding us of that, to show us the right thing to do, and to give us the fortitude to deal with the problems life throws at us.'

JANE, BIRMINGHAM, UK

Angels to set you on the right path

Decisions can be difficult to make — the choices are rarely clear-cut. If they were, it would be easy to make up our minds. Access your angel oracle to help you choose the right path.

Finding an angel to direct your way

When you have decisions and life choices to make, it can be a very difficult time. Should you move house, change your job, break up with your partner or enter into a new relationship?

What makes it especially hard is that your decision is unlikely to affect you alone; it probably involves your whole family, colleagues or friends. You might easily choose one option if it did not impact so heavily on someone else, or you could have difficulty choosing between two options with equal but different disadvantages.

Perhaps you don't have all the information you need to make your decision. This makes things harder, particularly if you know that information will not be available in time for it to help you. It can lead to your thoughts going round in circles because you lack that missing piece to help you choose a path.

Again, you may know the right choice but be afraid to make it. Some decisions are painful whatever you do. And if it is case of choosing what is right for you in the knowledge that someone else will not be happy about your decision, that makes it especially hard. Finally, you may be suffering from the problem of 'I used to be decisive, but I'm not so sure now'. It can simply be difficult to make up your mind.

It is not easy to learn to make honest decisions bravely, but it is something we all must do throughout our lives. In this section we will focus on the energy of Sandalphon to help you find the right path.

Because he was once human, Sandalphon understands first hand the difficulties we can face, and his responsibility for weaving the prayers of humans into flowers then taking them to God means that he has experience of the things we find most difficult and knows where we need the most help. If we can get in touch with the inner link to the angel we can bring his energy to support our own. He can help us to identify the fears that are holding us back and show us how to break away from them and move forward in the right direction.

Use a map to find your path

If you have a relatively straightforward decision to make but are still finding it hard, one effective method of finding the right path to take is to think of your decision in terms of a map. You should be beginning to grow comfortable with the relaxation process, so we will repeat only a simplified version here. The full process is described on pages 58–62.

You will need to choose suitable correspondences to help you access Sandalphon's energies. For Earth associations, you might use a white or dark-orange crystal, with a fragrant sandalwood candle surrounded with sand. Sandalphon is often associated with soothing

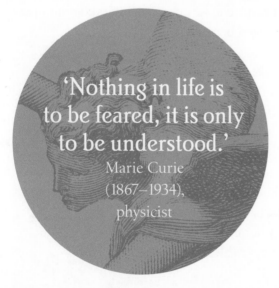

'Nothing in life is to be feared, it is only to be understood.'
Marie Curie
(1867–1934),
physicist

music, so you may like to put on a quiet and melodious CD. You will also need a sheet of paper and two coloured pens.

* Start with a relaxation session to encourage you to connect with your inner angel, in this case Sandalphon.

* Make yourself comfortable, practise your deep breathing, stretch then relax your muscles and let your mind follow suit.

* Focus your mind on the qualities Sandalphon can bring to your decision-making, encapsulating them in his image, if you wish.

* Now bring your mind into focus just enough to think about the circumstances you are in, but avoiding the temptation to let logic take over. Allow your intuition to guide you.

* Take the paper and write at the bottom the situation you are in now. Draw two or more roads on your paper, depending on how many options you have. Now write at the start of each path the first decision you will need to make in order to follow that path.

* One at a time, follow each road, writing down what you might find along the way, other opportunities or side roads that could open up for you.

* Don't think too hard about what you are writing; let your intuition take over and just brainstorm the ideas that come into your head.

'When your values are clear to you, making decisions becomes easier.'
Roy E. Disney (1930–2009), nephew of Walt Disney and senior executive of The Walt Disney Company

* When you feel that your conscious mind is intruding too much, stop writing and focus once again on Sandalphon. Bring his energy into your mental image of the angel, then absorb it into yourself.

* Now bring yourself back to reality, taking the new energy with you, and look at what you have written.

* Is it clear which path you would like to choose? Your chosen route is likely to be much more detailed and interesting.

* Take a pen of a different colour and bring logic to bear. Add the actions you need to take now that your path is clear.

* Always remember that, having made your choice, things will not happen of their own accord so take action to put your decisions into practice.

Facing our fears

If it is not choosing which way to move forward that you are finding difficult, perhaps there is something holding you back. Making a decision involves change, which can often be unnerving. You may need strength to overcome your fears.

Think about what you are afraid of; if it is more than one thing, take each one individually. Write it down, if that helps. Bring Sandalphon into your mind and ask for his help in making your decision. Relax and tune into your inner angel. Then ask yourself: 'What's the worst that could happen?'

Sometimes, there may be a serious consequence that will require much thinking to resolve. In such circumstances, you will need to find your inner strength. I suggest you adapt the Camael meditation on page 173 to favour Sandalphon, or simply use it as it stands.

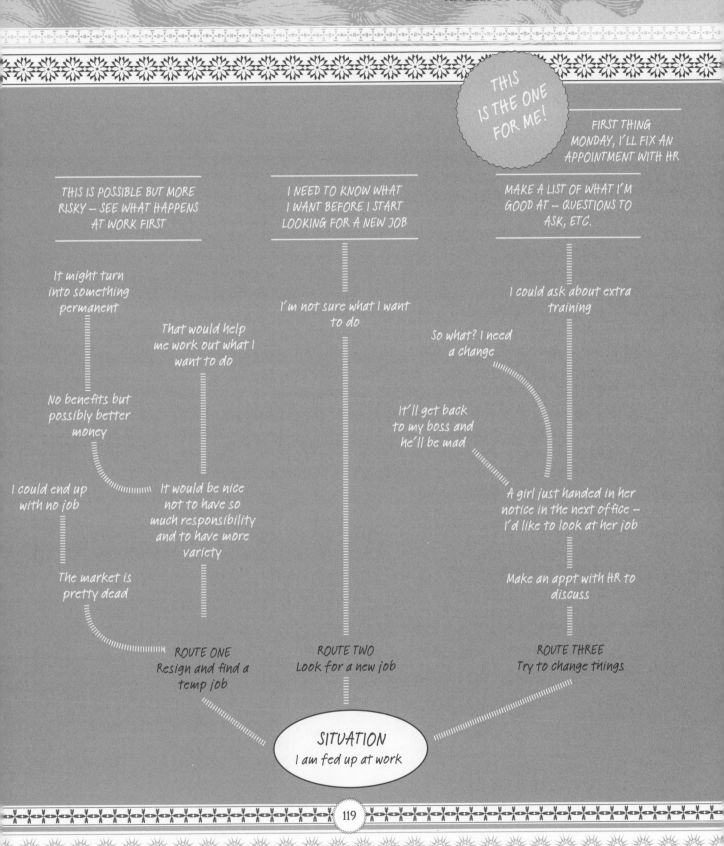

THIS IS THE ONE FOR ME!

FIRST THING MONDAY, I'LL FIX AN APPOINTMENT WITH HR

THIS IS POSSIBLE BUT MORE RISKY – SEE WHAT HAPPENS AT WORK FIRST

I NEED TO KNOW WHAT I WANT BEFORE I START LOOKING FOR A NEW JOB

MAKE A LIST OF WHAT I'M GOOD AT – QUESTIONS TO ASK, ETC.

It might turn into something permanent

I could ask about extra training

That would help me work out what I want to do

I'm not sure what I want to do

So what? I need a change

No benefits but possibly better money

It'll get back to my boss and he'll be mad

I could end up with no job

It would be nice not to have so much responsibility and to have more variety

A girl just handed in her notice in the next office – I'd like to look at her job

The market is pretty dead

Make an appt with HR to discuss

ROUTE ONE
Resign and find a temp job

ROUTE TWO
Look for a new job

ROUTE THREE
Try to change things

SITUATION
I am fed up at work

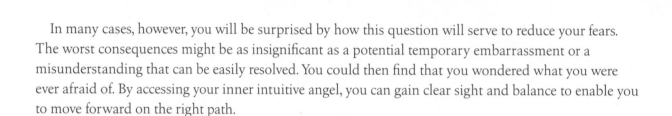

In many cases, however, you will be surprised by how this question will serve to reduce your fears. The worst consequences might be as insignificant as a potential temporary embarrassment or a misunderstanding that can be easily resolved. You could then find that you wondered what you were ever afraid of. By accessing your inner intuitive angel, you can gain clear sight and balance to enable you to move forward on the right path.

Using angel cards

Decision-making can also be facilitated by using angel cards. They offer a way of communicating with your inner angel to find out those things that you are unwilling to admit to, even to yourself.

There are many sets of cards commercially available. The set that is right for you is the one that attracts you by its colour and style, that feels right in your hands. Don't buy a set you are not sure of – it will be the wrong one. The instructions may vary with different sets of cards, as there are a number of layouts associated with the Tarot spreads and these are also often used for angel readings. The layout on the right is the simplest spread, which is designed to help you think about a course of action. However, you may prefer to use another layout and, again, go with what you feel is right.

You will need a set of angel cards, purchased or home-made, and your supporting correspondences – perhaps an orange or white selenite crystal and a sandalwood fragrance. There are ideas on pages 156–159 if you wish to make your own cards.

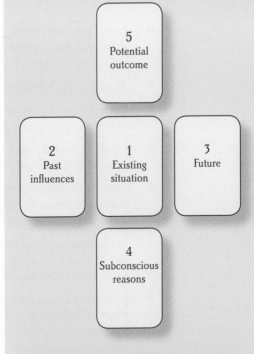

* Find the right time and place and light your candles or incense.

* Go through your relaxation process and take the cards face down in your hands. Hold them for a few moments. Bring the image of Sandalphon into your mind, or another angel who is appropriate.

* Concentrate on the issue in hand, focusing on the most important aspect. If your focus is too broad, it will be hard to interpret the cards.

* Shuffle the cards and lay the first five face down in a diamond shape, with the first card in the centre (see diagram above right).

* Once you have laid them out, refresh the image of Sandalphon in your mind and let your instinct guide you.

* Turn over card 1, in the centre, which represents the situation as it stands. Think about how the message on the card sheds angel light on your instinctive feelings about your circumstances.

* Now turn over card 2, on the left, which represents the main influences that have been active in bringing you to this position. Knowing why you are where you are is the first step in moving on.

* Turn over card 3, on the right, to meditate on your future course of action.

* Turn over card 4, at the bottom, which should shed some light on the subconscious reason for your problem; perhaps something that has been holding you back.

* Finally, turn over card 5, at the top, and consider the angel message in relation to the potential outcome of your actions.

* Spend a little time considering the energies the angel on each card represents and how you could use them to your advantage in finding the right path to follow. This may force you into some lateral thinking.

* Make sure you hold on to the energy and support you found in the image of Sandalphon when you bring your concentration back to reality.

* Focus on looking into your heart to access the inner understanding of what is best for you, and use your understanding to banish negative thoughts and arrive at a balanced decision. If you are beginning to tune into your inner angel oracle, you will find that any of these pure energies will strengthen and guide you in the right direction. Whatever the direction of the source of the light, it will light your way.

Setting you on the right path

Many cultures have their own ways of helping people make decisions. In Bolivia, the people buy llama amulets from the local wise woman. She activates the amulet for the recipient by winding a length of llama wool around its neck so that it knows how to guide you on the right path.

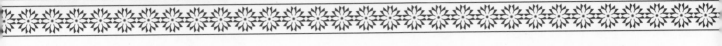

Angels help me with little miracles …'

'I was 18 years old when this happened. It's a small story but I have told plenty of people and it makes them smile…

'I was following my friend home from school in my car as we were going to do a school project together. I followed him to an intersection where we were turning left. The road was busy so he turned but I had to wait for a gap in the traffic. When I turned into the road, I drove slowly, checking whether my friend had pulled into one of the parking bays to wait for me, but I couldn't see him. Just when I was beginning to freak out I saw what I thought was his car and followed it into an area I didn't know before I realized it was not his car. I felt angry and frustrated, and even a little scared, so I decided to pull over to regain my bearings.

'I knew my phone was out of battery but I turned it on all the same – and it worked! I found the street name, then rang and told my mom my problem and she went to look up the map for where I told her I was, but just before she could tell me, I lost the phone connection. I called again and, once again, I was relieved that it worked just long enough to tell me the street was not on the map. Then the phone died again. I was fed up by this time. I thought I had nothing to lose by trying once more – and once again I got through. I told mom I was going to go home and then it died for the third and last time.

'As I drove off to retrace my way back, I passed a church and said a prayer: "just let me find my friend, let me get to his house; we have to do this project!" For some reason I felt compelled to look to my left and what did I see but my friend headed in the opposite direction! I quickly turned around and followed him to his house, which I had actually passed in my little adventure. I told him what had happened and that I thought God and his angels help people more than they realize, because you are not always at a church when these little miracles happen.'

GALYNN, CALIFORNIA, USA

Angels to bring you calm

'Take rest; a field that has rested gives a bountiful crop.'
Ovid (43BC–AD18),
poet and philosopher

A certain amount of pressure can help to bring out the best in us, but unrealistic expectations may stress us out and wear us down. Summon the energy of the archangel Anael to help relieve the tension.

Finding an angel to restore your equilibrium

Stress is increasingly a feature of modern life, to such an extent that even very young people claim to be 'stressed out' – an expression that has become part of the language.

A certain amount of pressure can be useful as it motivates us to try harder and do better. There's nothing like a deadline to encourage us to finish a piece of work, or the imminent arrival of visitors to make us clean the house.

However, some external pressures can tip the balance and cause us to feel unwell. These might include managing finances in increasingly difficult times; expectations at work; health issues; or the pressures of studying. Many stresses are self-inflicted, perhaps because we expect too much of ourselves or of life. If we subscribe to the modern cult of celebrity and think we need, for example, a celebrity-style wedding or to live life in the fast lane, then stress and disappointment are inevitable. At its best, stress is a great motivator; at worst, it can make us physically and mentally ill.

At such times, we need to take control of the pressure so that it doesn't spiral out of control. We have to restore calm and balance and change our attitude to the situation around us – this isn't easy. The help of an angel is invaluable in finding the strength to relieve your anxiety and restore balance in your

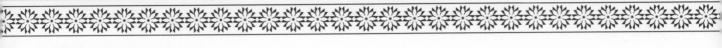

stress levels. Anael can foster an atmosphere of calm by surrounding us with love and healing. He will help remove the abrasive atmosphere of stress and bring a feeling of tranquillity; he will restore your strength and allow you to find your own way of coping with the pressures of your circumstances.

Remember, however, that these suggestions relate to ordinary, everyday stresses, not to serious mental health issues such as depression. With all issues of mental health, you will rarely benefit from keeping them to yourself. There is a certain stigma associated with mental health that does not exist in relation to physical illnesses. But there is nothing shameful in suffering serious consequences of stress; on the contrary, it takes a strong person to admit to them and look for help. If for any reason you feel control is slipping away from you, you should always seek professional advice rather than rely on self help.

Calm in the clouds

Extreme anxiety tips your life out of its natural balance, which needs to be restored. You may find simple relaxation helps, or you may need a different routine. Call on the calming energies of Anael to restore your peace of mind.

If you wish, you can hold a rose or a rose-coloured crystal, but this is not essential. This is an outdoor exercise that is ideally performed on a cloudy and slightly breezy day. It doesn't matter whether there are many clouds or only a few. Cumulus, stratus or cirrus will all be fine, although storm clouds are not a good focus for a calming activity.

If you can find a place near the the sound of running water for this exercise so much the better, as this will bring Water energies into your scope.

❊ Make yourself comfortable, as usual, ensuring you have a clear view of the sky. Hold your crystal in your hand, if you wish.

❊ Breathe deeply as you watch the clouds roll by overhead. Observe them closely and allow your mind to focus on them completely. Imagine that you can see Anael hovering above you.

❊ Follow your inclination. You may find you prefer to look for patterns or images in the clouds. Your concentration should help you put aside thoughts of the things that are upsetting your equanimity so that your calm is restored.

'Do not anticipate trouble or worry about what may never happen. Keep in the sunlight.'
Benjamin Franklin, (1706–1790), US president

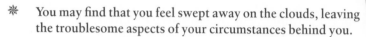

> 'Inward calm cannot be maintained unless physical strength is constantly and intelligently replenished.'
> Buddha (563–483BC)

* You may find that you feel swept away on the clouds, leaving the troublesome aspects of your circumstances behind you.

* Indulge in the feeling as long as you can, then bring your focus back to Anael. Watch his light being drawn into your own inner oracle, then bring that energy back with you to reality.

Balancing the equation

Of course, when you are back in the everyday world, the cause of your stress will almost certainly still be waiting for you. Meditate on Anael to help alleviate this.

* You will need two small bowls, ideally pink and green, and some tokens – tiddlywinks, coloured sweets or baking beans.

* Find a convenient time and place, and relax.

* Think about the calming and balancing energies of Anael and ask for help in maintaining your own balance.

* Let your intuition guide you towards the thing that stresses you out the most. It is likely to be the first thing that comes into your head but, even so, it may take you by surprise. Your subconscious will guide you to the root cause. Put a token in the green bowl to represent this element.

* Now let your mind suggest things you could do to combat, minimize or resolve the problem. Try to remain detached as you visualize actions you could take. For each idea that crosses your mind, put a token in the pink bowl. You may feel some problems or solutions deserve more than one token.

* You may wish to move on to other difficulties, but it is best not to deal with too much at once. This could lead to confusion, which could lead to more, not less, stress.

* Allow your intuition to guide you as far as possible, then bring your conscious mind back into play.

* You may already find you have a choice of new, positive ideas that you can think about putting into practice. That's excellent, but don't rush headlong into everything; take your time.

If the negatives still outweigh the positives, it may be that there are too many things to change straightaway. These issues are part of your life – at least for now – so you will have to find coping strategies. This involves lateral thinking – looking for ways round the problem or ways of changing your attitude to it. If you are struggling with the restrictions of a long working day, perhaps you can make life a bit easier by asking another member of the family to have supper on the table when you get home. If your boss unfairly favours a particular member of staff over you, see this as his or her problem, not yours.

Stopping stress in its tracks

Once you recognize the triggers that start to send your stress levels skyrocketing, watch for the early signs and take steps to prevent the negative energies overwelming you. There are many methods you can try – experiment with them until you find what works best for you, then try to devise a short-cut to apply when you feel creeping anxiety. This may involve taking some action, repeating a mantra or some other routine. All these methods are designed to clear your mind of stressful things. Look to your inner oracle to know which route is best for you.

Physical activity can be very effective: running, walking, swimming, or any sports you enjoy. Immerse yourself in the physical and give your mental dimension a break so that you can return to your problem-solving later on.

✳ Counting or other repetitive exercises can bring tranquillity by forcing your mind to abandon that which is making you feel anxious.

✳ Practical tasks can be effective – try doing some baking or mowing the lawn.

✳ Talk to someone who is prepared to listen attentively.

✳ Try popping a piece of bubble wrap, moulding plasticine or squeezing a stress ball.

✳ Listen to soothing music.

✳ Have a warm bath with a few drops of relaxing lavender or ylang ylang oil added.

✳ Indulge in a body or head massage or a similar treatment.

✳ Laughter is not usually spontaneous when you are stressed, but a light-hearted comedy film may be just what you need to make you smile or, better still, laugh.

'If you don't like something, change it; if you can't change it, change the way you think about it.'
Mary Engelbreit (b. 1952), children's book illustrator

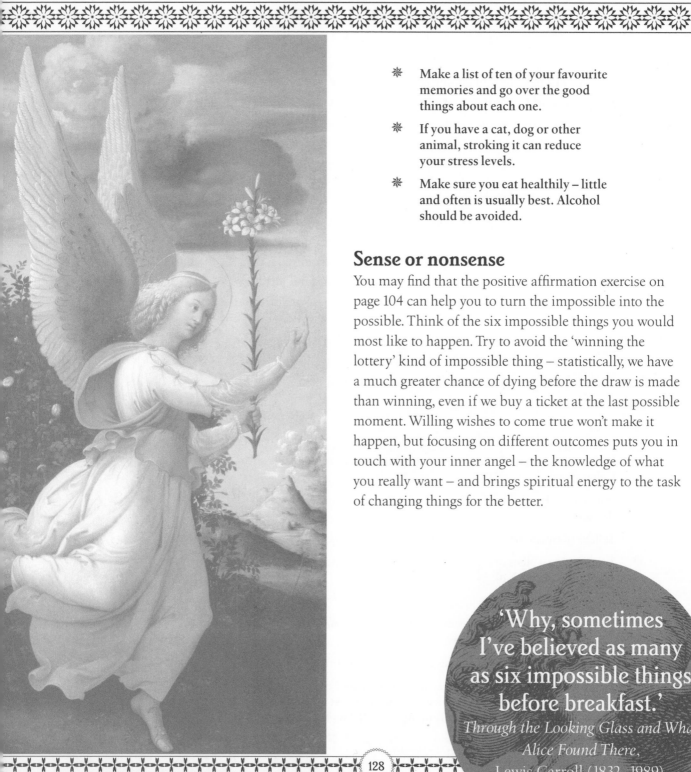

* Make a list of ten of your favourite memories and go over the good things about each one.

* If you have a cat, dog or other animal, stroking it can reduce your stress levels.

* Make sure you eat healthily – little and often is usually best. Alcohol should be avoided.

Sense or nonsense

You may find that the positive affirmation exercise on page 104 can help you to turn the impossible into the possible. Think of the six impossible things you would most like to happen. Try to avoid the 'winning the lottery' kind of impossible thing – statistically, we have a much greater chance of dying before the draw is made than winning, even if we buy a ticket at the last possible moment. Willing wishes to come true won't make it happen, but focusing on different outcomes puts you in touch with your inner angel – the knowledge of what you really want – and brings spiritual energy to the task of changing things for the better.

'Why, sometimes I've believed as many as six impossible things before breakfast.'
Through the Looking Glass and What Alice Found There, Lewis Carroll (1832–1989), author

'An angel helped me when I was on the verge of tears...'

'Angels are an unforgettable reminder that God truly cares about every detail of our lives. Until recently only my family and a few friends had ever heard my rainy day angel story.

'I am visually impaired. I do have some sight, but a lot of things affect it – the time of day, how bright the sun is, how much contrast is in the environment and so on. I was out on the street on an incredibly rainy winter day. Although it was only 3.30, it was getting dark. I fear the dusk more than anything because I can see far better at night than when it is dusk. I was trying to get to a pharmacy where I paid my utility bill. It was past due and I wanted to get it taken care of that day, but I couldn't find my way. I was totally disoriented, although I'd been to that place a hundred times.

'The way the area was paved made it hard for me to tell which was the sidewalk and which was the street. I was soaked to the skin, confused and on the verge of tears. I'm quite an independent person but there seemed to be no way getting myself out of this one. When I was nearly mowed down by a car, I stopped to pray. I hadn't even finished with the prayer when I heard a robust man's voice.

'"Can I help you?" he asked.

'I looked up at him. He looked to be in his early 60s or late 50s. He was wearing a blue raincoat and a blue baseball cap. I think he had a patch on one shoulder. It looked like a postman's uniform. He had a ruddy, bronze complexion with a shock of white hair just above the roll of flesh on the back of his neck. Looking back, I think he mostly looks like a rainy day angel.

'I hated asking for help because people get carried away and ask a lot of irrelevant questions until I'm overwhelmed.

'"I'm trying to get to Beaverton Pharmacy." I said. "I've got to get there before they close."

'"Oh, I know where that is," he said cheerfully.

'"Here it comes!" I thought. "Now I'll never get rid of him."

'Then he did the most amazing thing. He turned away from me and offered me his elbow. I about fell over. My own parents still try to push me ahead of them if they think I need guidance. Even my boyfriend didn't know how to guide me.

'I took his arm. It was warm and surprisingly dry. As we walked, I started rattling away about how I got myself into this predicament – I needed to just be heard without being told what to do or what I should have done or having to answer the question "How many fingers am I holding up?"

'The man never said another word; he just listened. I had a profound and growing sense that this man knew me very well. He knew me better than anyone else I know. I wondered if it was an older man from my church, there was no doubt he knew everything about me.

'When we rounded a corner, I recognized where we were.

'"Oh, thanks! I know where I am now," I said. As I let go of his arm, I turned to thank him. No one was there, just the rain. There were no footsteps leading away, not even a shadow.

'It seemed I stood there for the longest time, trying to comprehend what had just happened, which was as real as everything else around me. When I thought about it, I hadn't heard any footsteps coming toward me when I was praying. I had been a little startled, in fact, because he seemed to just – appear. Tears welled up in my eyes and I felt like the reality of it might pull me to the ground – that God had sent an angel to help me.

'I think I've seen him one other time, possibly two. I'm pretty certain about the second time. He was walking with a lady. I had a guide dog by this time, but I still sometimes get disoriented. He gave me the directions I asked for, then vanished.

'Both times, my awareness of this being a supernatural experience was hidden until after the fact. I think God does this in order to not draw attention away from what is more important. It's not really about meeting an angel. It is about God sending me exactly what I needed.'

SHELLEY, USA

Angels to help you grow

You are never too old to learn; discovering new things keeps us active and alive. We should embrace challenges as part of life — this is easy to say, but harder to put into practice. Look to the angels to help in the quest to broaden your mind.

Finding an angel to expand your horizons

Our physical, mental and spiritual well-being is improved when we maintain an open and enquiring mind, so we should never give up trying to keep abreast of news, local and international activities, friends and family.

If you are in the middle of studying – whether at school, university or in professional or work-based training – it can be a pretty demanding time and you may need all the support you can muster. For those who know they should take up a new interest or hobby, start a course or do some on-the-job training, it can feel as though getting round to it requires too much energy . . . and time slips by. On top of this, broadening your outlook involves change. This can be daunting, which is surprising since it is, in fact, the only thing in life that is certain. Nothing on this earth stays the same. Life takes us with it on its natural, never-ending cycle.

If you are trying to broaden your outlook by participating in an evening class, joining a club, working at organizing your life more efficiently or making new

'Education is the best provision for the journey to old age.'
Aristotle (384–322 BC), philosopher

friends, all these things can be energy sapping. In these circumstances you can get a boost by calling on Metatron's energies to help you. His virtues include all aspects of learning: understanding, logical thought and organization, together with spiritual knowledge. He is ideal to help us when we want to broaden our outlook, to grow and to learn.

Your own tree of life

As the guardian of the tree of life, Metatron reminds us that everything in this world, and beyond, is inextricably linked. The most common symbol of the tree of life is based on the flower of life, a kabbalistic, geometric structure created of even, interconnected circles – a clear visual representation of the interdependency of all living things.

Create your own drawing of the tree of life as a basis for growing your interests or developing your learning opportunities. Your tree does not have to be as complex or perfect as the one illustrated – you may prefer a representative drawing to a geometric one. A simple drawing of a tree to which you can add leaves representing your achievements would work well. If you are artistically gifted, you might like to model your drawing on the whole flower of life, especially if your study or growth is more likely to be expansive rather than linear. Appropriate correspondences to enliven the energy around you might be a cedarwood candle, for fragrance and to represent the Fire element, and perhaps one or two dark red crystals, such as red aventurine or sardonyx.

❋ You will need your chosen correspondences, a clean sheet of paper, a ruler or straight edge, a pair of compasses or a cup to draw round and a maroon cloth.

❋ Find a suitable time and place. Spread the cloth on a table and prepare whatever correspondences you may be using.

❋ Relax, then bring the image of Metatron into your mind and hold it there.

❋ Start by copying a simple version of the basic structure of your tree, letting your intuition be your guide. For the tree of life, begin by drawing three circles in a triangle at the bottom of the paper.

❋ Write in, or next to the first circle the qualifications you have, or the level you have reached, then add into each of the remaining circles the qualifications you could obtain, or the activities you could be involved in. Draw lines or arrows to show the most logical sequence from one to the other. Then add more circles as you see yourself progressing; they don't have to mirror the pattern of the classic tree of life.

❋ Once you have completed your tree, look at it carefully and search your inner oracle to decide what it is you want to achieve. Rely on the energy of Metatron, which you can bring to play on the questions you are asking. Keep it with you as you complete the exercise.

❋ Finally, start to devise ways of making your proposals come to fruition. Bring Metatron's energy back to your everyday life and use his image as a focus to help you.

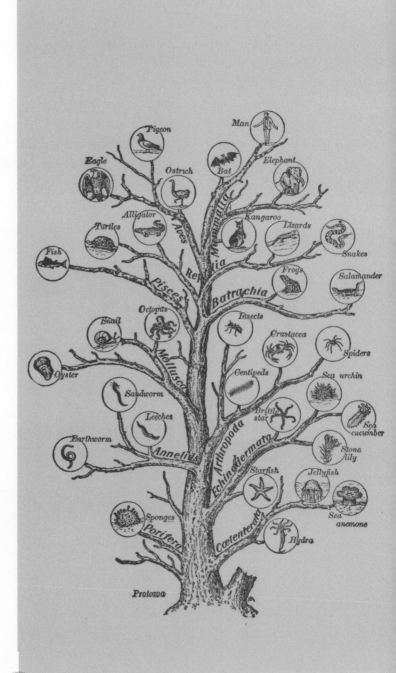

Growing towards others

In many of these exercises, the focus has been on the self, for it is undeniable that we can only change ourselves and not others. However, growing our spiritual core by helping others is hugely important both to ourselves and to society as a whole.

We can mirror the tree of life exercise using another sacred geometric figure, Metatron's Cube. This is comprised of 12 equal circles surrounding a central circle and is perfectly linked together. This is often used for cleansing the chakras to free up spiritual energy. In this exercise it is used as a model for the positive influence you can have on those around you.

You will need paper and pencil, as well as your chosen correspondences – myrrh fragrance would work well.

'We cannot teach people anything, we can only help them discover it within themselves.'
Galileo Galilei (1564–1642), scientist

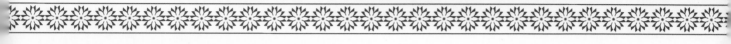

※ In a suitable time and place, burn your fragrance, if you are using one, and make yourself comfortable. Relax and bring the image of Metatron into your mind and try to put away any other thoughts. Let your intuition guide you.

※ Visualize Metatron's Cube as a cube of light entering through your crown chakra and moving down through the chakra points, flushing out any negative energy.

※ Without applying your conscious mind, draw a circle in the centre of the paper to represent yourself. Write on it, or near it, the qualities you can share with other people that would help you to grow by assisting others.

※ Begin to add circles round the circumference of the circle – like the ones at the centre of Metatron's Cube (opposite) – to indicate the people you might touch. It may be that you will get involved in voluntary work or help others in a direct way. Perhaps you will benefit your family by gaining a qualification to increase your income; you may be able to advise friends on new computer programs because you have taken a course at work; your employment opportunities may be broadened by taking an evening course, thereby reducing the pressure on your partner to work quite so hard.

※ Join the circles with lines to indicate the links between the different people and the activities you are engaged in.

Undoubtedly, it will look rather random and uneven – unlike the model cube – but it will have focused your mind on the ripple effect for good brought about by your efforts to reach out to others. It should help you feel stronger by emphasizing your links with others and the supportive network that this creates.

Growing a tree of life

If you have a garden, or even a windowsill, you can grow a plant to represent your tree of life and watch it grow in parallel with your efforts to learn and expand your knowledge. The tree will be there to promote your successes or chide your backsliding! Of course, it doesn't have to be a tree, although a bonsai tree indoors or a small tree or shrub outdoors would be appropriate. You will need to fit nature to circumstance. If you only have a room or a small flat, a little pot of herbs with do just as well to represent your efforts to grow.

Care for your plant as you work on growing and developing your intellectual abilities, expanding your social network or embarking on new projects. When you feed and water it, think about whether you have spent an appropriate amount of time on your studies or activities. Perhaps you may need to trim it back from time to time. If it is a culinary herb, you should also be using it to your advantage, as you need to find ways to make use of your new-found knowledge.

All these activities will help keep you in daily touch with your inner angel because they will make you think about what is best for you and what can make you the best person you can be.

> 'Good actions give strength to ourselves and inspire good actions in others.'
>
> Plato (424–348BC), philosopher

A target within your reach

Setting targets is a good way to motivate yourself to achieve your goals, but remember that targets should always be realistic. Don't set yourself a target you are already on the way to achieving, which is therefore a safe bet. This will not test your resolve and may make you complacent. At the other end of the scale, you should not aim for something you know is impossible to achieve.

The middle way – as usual – is the right one. Think hard, meditate on your angel, and think about what is possible for you to achieve with dedication and commitment. That is the target to go for.

'Angels help me learn...'

'If life takes an unexpected turn, I have learnt to surrender and trust that sometimes a greater purpose is being served at that moment than my individual expectations. The divine allows free will, choice and consequence, but never without guidance to assist us in making choices that will allow our lives to flow more smoothly. When I ask for this guidance, I receive it.

'I believe we will all have learning experiences, but if you embrace them, your life will tend towards greater and greater ease and joy. Ask for assistance, pray, and you will be at peace. The divine supports us and guides us when we ask for this and are willing to receive.'

BEVERLEY, MASSACHUSETTS, USA

Angels to help you change

Habits are harder to break than principles — so the old saying goes. Looking for spiritual help can strengthen our resolve and give us the willpower and energy to make changes for the better.

The potential in change

Change is not always easy to embrace even though, as we have said before, it is one of the only certainties in life. While the angel on one shoulder could be telling us to spread our wings, the angel on the other shoulder could be instructing us to stay where we are. We tend to like the things we are used to – they are comfortable and secure, like a pair of old shoes. But if we just keep on wearing them, they will eventually fall apart. How much better to have a new pair that you have started to break in, than suddenly to have nothing and be forced to start again from the beginning.

Change is inevitable; learn to grasp it, or even pre-empt it and make it happen sooner rather than later. Angelic inspiration can help you to concentrate and broaden your mind so that you can identify potential in all things and have the courage to embrace it. If you want to change your job, lose weight, stop smoking or change bad habits, settle down and focus on what your inner angel is trying to tell you. When his wife was tragically killed, Kevin Skelton was devastated and began drinking heavily. But he could feel the angelic spirit of his wife, Mina, and he believes she was his angel who gave him the strength to turn his life around.

The angel of transformation, Uriel, is the focus to shed light when you need to make changes. He understands the cycle of life through birth, growth, death and rebirth, and by bringing his energies into our sphere of influence we can use him to help us adapt to evolving circumstances. If we tap into our inner understanding, we will see the logic of the circle and the importance of the ever-moving process. Things that stay the same for too long will stagnate; things that rush forward headlong can be destructive. Only with balance can we retain the optimum motion.

From caterpillar to butterfly

The classic image of metamorphosis in the natural world is the transformation from caterpillar to chrysalis to butterfly, stages in a life cycle of a single creature that turns itself from one being into another. Even if the alchemists had succeeded in turning base metal into gold, it would have been a mundane transformation by comparison.

So, if we look at this lifecycle pattern, perhaps we can use it to help reproduce a similarly startling, if very different, kind of change.

You will need to choose correspondences, starting with a dark red candle in a brass or gold-coloured dish, if you have one. You could choose a candle with a lemon fragrance if you feel in need of stimulation, or sandalwood if you feel a soothing aroma is more appropriate. Surround the candle with red-brown crystals such as haematite, rutilated quartz or tiger's eye to bring both their own qualities of strength and mental stimulation, and also to represent the element of Earth.

※ Light the candle, and relax in a comfortable place. Breathe deeply, relax and bring the image of Uriel to your mind. Focus on your deep, intuitive knowledge of what is right for you.

※ Begin as the hungry caterpillar, whose sole purpose is to build up reserves of energy. Nothing else matters, because change requires energy, both spiritual and physical, in order to take place.

※ Look back for a moment. Identify things in your life that have not worked for you or that you don't like doing: missed opportunities, hurtful moments, wrong choices. As you watch them pass by you, acknowledge that they are in the past and there is nothing you can do about them. Forget them. Let them go. It is only the good times that are worth remembering.

※ Feel the energy boost when you cut the strings that you have been allowing to hold you back. Feed on that spiritual energy.

※ Now, in your mind, retreat into your cocoon. Use that newly acquired energy to recognize that you are at a tipping point and you can take control. Think about the best times in your life and start to use the positive energy. Think about simple joys and let this thought give you the strength to make changes.

※ Finally, emerge from your cocoon with renewed strength, ready to implement the changes you need to make in order to have the life you deserve. You are in control of producing the results you want from now, so keep talking to your inner angel, who can tell you intuitively what the best thing is for you. Store the angelic energy in your image of Uriel to call upon when you need it most.

Following the best examples

It's easy to compare yourself favourably with people who are 'worse' than you (she's fatter, so I'm not so bad; he never buys the coffee, so I'm more generous). To be honest, sometimes it does help when we are being particularly hard on ourselves. It is not healthy to put ourselves down all the time; it is essential to maintain a balance. But if we want to make changes, it is far better to look at the people you most admire and identify traits you would like to emulate.

If you are going to change, find yourself the right role models. Looking at the way they have achieved success in whatever form will give you a blueprint from which you can take encouragement.

Never follow other people slavishly. What is right for someone else is not necessarily right for you. But look at their actions and their attitude for inspiration. Chances are that they have set themselves attainable goals, worked hard, grasped opportunities with both hands and, above all, believed in themselves and their ability to take control and make things happen. They are in touch with their inner angel.

'An angel changed my life...'

'I made this diary entry a decade after I had an experience I'll never forget that changed my life and the way I perceived it permanently. It still affects me to this day. I don't ask that anyone believe it, some may even think it's only a dream, but I know better...

'As a 16-year-old boy, I lived with my family on a large farm and dairy in an isolated valley near the Idaho/Utah boarder. We had our ups and downs but, for the most part, we were very close and worked very hard together.

'I had gone to bed on an autumn night and, while in a deep sleep, I heard someone call my name three times, each time more urgently. As I sat up, I did not expect to see what was before my eyes: a young man who looked very familiar, with brown wavy hair, green eyes, and a deep light emanating from within him that made his being shine, and the light that surrounded him lit my room. It didn't frighten me. He stood as though on solid ground but was not touching the floor. He was dressed in a white, robe-like garment. I looked behind me and saw that I was sitting up out of my body, which was still lying in the bed.

'The visitor held out his hand and beckoned me to take it and come with him because he had something he needed to share with me. He communicated only by thought; I felt what he said in my heart, but it sounded like vocal communication, although it had more depth, and you could feel the emotion and urgency of his message.

'So I took his hand and, in an instant, we travelled by thought, appearing by each of my family members' beds. He spoke of past events, of what was happening now and where it all would lead in the future. He did this for each member, both parent and sibling, and told me how they fitted into the picture. Then he showed me where, when and how I was to intervene.

'The things he told me, I still carry with me, but they only come to me when the time and situation is perfect. He told me this is the way it would be, because all that he shared would overwhelm me if I were to remember all of it at once.

'Before my visitor left me, we appeared back in my bedroom. He took both my hands, looked me in the eyes with a piercing brilliance of pure love and energy, and said, "It's up to you now. You must keep this family together, love them, and teach them what I tell

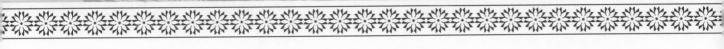

you, when the time is right." Then he embraced me and we both wept. Then he released me and I laid back into my body. I jumped from my bed and knelt down beside it and cried, "God, why me? Why did this happen to me? Why is this my responsibility?". Then a calming peace came over me and I felt everything would be all right. But the love and purity of the light of the angel still overwhelmed me, and I cried myself to sleep.

'Since then, many things have happened, and I somehow know exactly what to do, and how, and what to say. And I know where it's coming from. Like I said, many would scoff but it doesn't matter to me, I know what happened and how it changed me. I am glad of my experience and will always be thankful that someone cared enough to warn me so I could protect my family. '

JOHN, NEW YORK, USA

Angels to help you heal

Many people have experienced the benefits of angelic healing, through their own spiritual communication or with the help of a therapist who can teach them to open their spirits to angelic communication.

Finding an angel to bring you healing

Healing work with angels encompasses all kinds of circumstances, both physical and spiritual. The physical aspect is easy to define. If you are suffering from a health condition, whether acute or chronic, you need to deal with all the different issues that the absence of good health involves. The physical symptoms themselves can be difficult to cope with. You are likely to have less energy, and the energy you have has to be directed into rebuilding your damaged cells and perhaps into doing all kinds of practical things that other people do without thinking.

If your problems are mental, you may have to deal with the added stigma that mental health problems are not always as easily recognized or discussed as other health issues. Struggling with such problems demands physical energy. Although you may not be physically active, you can end up feeling drained and tired, even though your real problem is that you are hurting because a relationship has ended, or someone you love is ill, or you are involved in a serious and disruptive family argument.

Our general emotional well-being also comes into play, as sometimes we need to be healed of a sense of loss or betrayal following the breakdown of trust or the ensuing pain after an argument with a friend. We may need to defend ourselves against things that could have a negative effect on our physical or spiritual health, from viruses to people who try to impose their negative energies on us.

Healing can also relate to helping ourselves or helping others. It is painful to see someone we care for suffer, and it is very common for people to try

to find spiritual support in order to improve the lot of a friend or family member. If you want to help in this way, talk to the person first and give them time, sympathy and encouragement. That may be enough to give them the strength they need.

Healing is required in the broadest sense of the word throughout our lives. In this section it is to Raphael, the archangel of healing, that we look to focus our minds on finding the strength to restore our minds and bodies to health, or to support and help those who are close to us to return to good health.

Sending a gift of healing

Traditionally depicted as a pilgrim or traveller, Raphael is often shown carrying a golden phial of medicine and a bag of food for travellers. You can use these symbols to focus your healing energies on a gift for someone who is suffering.

Whether they are physically ill, or struggling with a relationship break-up, or having a difficult time for any other reason, you can personalize your gift to suit the

Don't expect miracles

Although people have reported unexplained cures for themselves or loved ones with serious medical conditions, this is never something you should expect, or even hope for. Disappointment is almost certain to be the result. We look to the angels for support, guidance and renewed energy. It may be in their gift to help us in many ways but we cannot predict how that may be. We can pray for renewed energy to face our circumstances, we can seek our innermost subconscious to find the best ways to cope, but hoping for too much is never a good option.

circumstances. What you are doing is showing them they are not alone and that you care about their situation enough to send them your energy to help them.

In each case, wrap your gift in green paper. Before you give your gift, hold it in your hands and meditate on the image of Raphael surrounded by a green light of healing. Focus on that light and, as you breathe deeply in and out, feel it spreading through your body and into the healing gift.

Here are some ideas for gifts you might give:

- ✳ Geraniums have the quality of regeneration, so present a geranium plant – in a pot or ready for the garden – to someone who is ill.

- ✳ Lily of the valley will boost and enliven the energies of someone who is ill or needs emotional healing.

- ✳ Lavender has a calming and soothing effect. From candles, incense and bath products to plants, lavender bags and dried lavender for cooking, there are hundreds of products to choose from. For a more personal touch, grow and make your own gifts.

- ✳ For those who are anxious or afraid, send a pot of thyme to keep by the bed or in the kitchen where it will waft its calming fragrance and be a reminder of the strength to be found in sharing with those who wish to help.

- ✳ Parsley has a cleansing effect, which might be suitable for someone with a health problem, whether that is a persistent virus or they need to be rid of something in their past that is holding them back.

- ✳ Herbal teas could also be suitable.

Plants energize the atmosphere and dispel negativity. Trinkets or items of jewellery using healing stones are also a positive way of sharing angel energies. Heart shapes are particularly appropriate as Raphael is associated with the heart chakra. Green is his primary colour, so try stones such as aventurine, beryl, chrysoprase, emerald, jade or malachite. Or you could try yellow stones such as citrine, honey calcite, fluorite or jasper.

Earth angels

People have reported being helped by friends or family in the most ordinary ways, but in a manner that was significant at the time, to such an extent that their actions helped the person turn a corner or begin their own process of healing. You may not consider yourself to be an angel but, with compassion and empathy, you can channel your positive energy to others in astonishing ways. It may be that you are simply sharing your own strength, or that you have become able to strengthen your own spirit with angelic power; either way, do not underestimate your power to do good, or overlook opportunities to put your power into action. You can do this by following the angelic example outlined on page 149.

✸ BE OBSERVANT Just as angels observe humans carefully to look out for their best interests, you can be observant of people around you and notice when they look down, are unwell or seem generally below par. It can be as simple as noticing when someone looks a bit pale or is not as chatty as usual. Observe their body language as well as what they say.

✸ BE THOUGHTFUL Try to put yourself in the position of others. Think what they might need, rather than what you might want to give them.

✸ COMMUNICATE There are so many methods of communication open to us that you can make your choice according to the circumstances. Anything from paying a visit, picking up the phone or sending a text to making a video call or sending an email, letter or card. Make contact. If you feel you have nothing special to say, find an appropriate card and use the old advertising slogan: 'I saw this and thought of you'. Hardly original, but why should that matter?

✸ OFFER PRACTICAL HELP Help someone up the stairs with a pushchair, or offer to pick up some shopping. When you are feeling down, the smallest lightening of your load can be hugely important, without it being an inconvenience to anyone else.

✸ BRING PEOPLE TOGETHER Recall a time when you were on your own in a group of people you didn't know. It's the loneliest place in the world! Introduce yourself to someone looking lost in an environment in which you are comfortable. You don't have to say anything amazingly original – the important thing is to include them in the circle.

✸ DON'T BE JUDGEMENTAL Many people have experienced both human and angelic help when they felt they were not performing at their best. Sometimes spiritual healing can be a turning point and may encourage a person to live a more altruistic life. Offer your healing energy without criticism of other people's decisions.

✸ OFFER A HEALING HUG A hug is the most amazing thing – sometimes nothing else will quite do to soothe your spirits, bring you comfort or make you feel better. Obviously, you should never 'force' a hug on anyone – that would be inappropriate – but if you are thoughtful and compassionate, you will be able to read the person's body language. In the event that you do judge the situation wrongly, simply step back immediately and apologize.

✸ SMILE Although we may cringe at the old cliché, 'If you see someone without a smile, give them one of yours', a smile is an easy way to make someone feel better. You don't have to go round grinning like a Cheshire cat, but there are times when you can lift someone's spirit with just a smile.

'That "hello" just meant so much...'

'I had just moved to a new area with a toddler and a tiny baby. I'd had precious little sleep, I didn't know a soul, my confidence was at the lowest ebb and I was feeling pretty lost. The baby was crying, my little girl was bored and I felt completely cut off.

'I had been invited to a coffee morning by a local mums' group but I really didn't feel I had the energy to get out of the house or face a room full of people I didn't know. But at the last minute, I managed to find some shreds of energy from somewhere and I set off.

'I arrived to find a room full of people chatting away. It felt as though they were all happy and confident and I was the only one who didn't know what she was doing. At that moment, it was my worst nightmare.

'Then a woman came up to me and said, "Hello. I haven't seen you here before," and proceeded to introduce herself to me and the girls. I have no idea what we said, only that I felt so relieved and grateful to be included. That "hello", at that moment, just meant so much to me. We are still friends 25 years later and I will never forget how we first met.'

ALICE, LONDON, UK

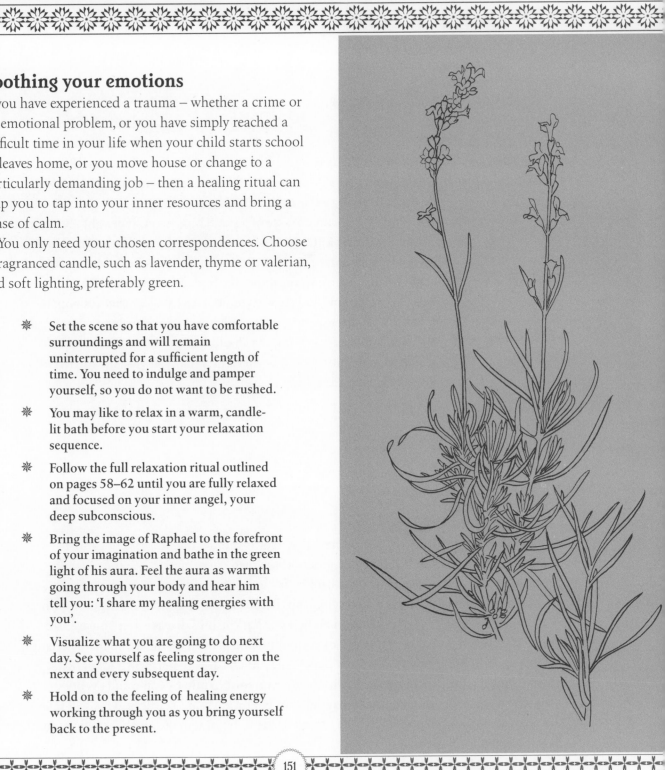

Soothing your emotions

If you have experienced a trauma – whether a crime or an emotional problem, or you have simply reached a difficult time in your life when your child starts school or leaves home, or you move house or change to a particularly demanding job – then a healing ritual can help you to tap into your inner resources and bring a sense of calm.

You only need your chosen correspondences. Choose a fragranced candle, such as lavender, thyme or valerian, and soft lighting, preferably green.

 Set the scene so that you have comfortable surroundings and will remain uninterrupted for a sufficient length of time. You need to indulge and pamper yourself, so you do not want to be rushed.

 You may like to relax in a warm, candle-lit bath before you start your relaxation sequence.

 Follow the full relaxation ritual outlined on pages 58–62 until you are fully relaxed and focused on your inner angel, your deep subconscious.

 Bring the image of Raphael to the forefront of your imagination and bathe in the green light of his aura. Feel the aura as warmth going through your body and hear him tell you: 'I share my healing energies with you'.

 Visualize what you are going to do next day. See yourself as feeling stronger on the next and every subsequent day.

 Hold on to the feeling of healing energy working through you as you bring yourself back to the present.

'An angel restored my hope...'

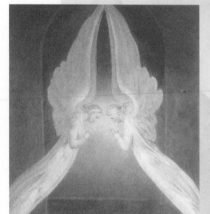

'I was in hospital the night before major surgery, the outcome of which was, at that time, very uncertain. Understandably, I was worried and my mind kept turning over all the possibilities – what if this? what if that? – so much so that sleep was impossible and I lay on the bed feeling exhausted but wide awake.

'Gradually I became aware of a small blue neon strip light above me – a bit like the fly killers that some food outlets used to have. I pinched myself to make sure I was definitely still awake. The light grew and changed shape until it was more like liquid seaside rock, which flowed down to me and curved round me a bit like a giant scoop. It was still that intense, bright neon blue and I felt enveloped in the light and absolutely sure – without a shadow of a doubt – that I was safe and that everything would be all right. Finally, I was able to drift off into a calm and refreshing sleep.'

DI, KENT, UK

Stay in control

A person suffering from a chronic illness may feel as though the illness is in control. Occasionally this is not helped by members of the medical profession, some of whom tend to define a patient by his or her disease. It can be distressing to hear about 'progress', if it means that the disease is progressing and therefore you, the patient, are getting worse.

You may be a person suffering from diabetes or Parkinson's disease, but you are still you. Try to keep that at the forefront of your mind and protest if you are not given credit for your abilities. A perfectly healthy person may not be able to perform a lot of tasks but no one draws attention to it. Maintain your interest in other people and events so that the hard work you put into managing your condition reaps rewards. This will take determination and energy – and many small battles – but it will be hugely beneficial to your spiritual well-being.

Angels to inspire you

'Our brightest blazes are commonly kindled by unexpected sparks.'
Samuel Johnson (1709–1784), author and commentator

A spiritual presence in our lives makes the mundane special, can heighten our creative abilities and helps us to exercise our talents — artistic or otherwise — to the maximum.

Finding an angel to light the spark

For those with faith in a higher power, whatever their religion, the ultimate inspiration comes from their god or supreme deity. Prayer opens up an interactive communication and is their inspiration for the way they lead their lives. Even those people, however, can find inspiration in the physical world around them to help broaden their scope and ensure that their creative abilities are stimulated and developed

Inspiration is most commonly associated with the creative arts and, indeed, creativity of that kind is a wonderful gift. But inspiration is broader than that. Angelic inspiration can enliven us in many different ways, whatever our talents, and encourage us to exercise those talents for the benefit of ourselves and others.

For those who already know that they love art and music, or know where they find their

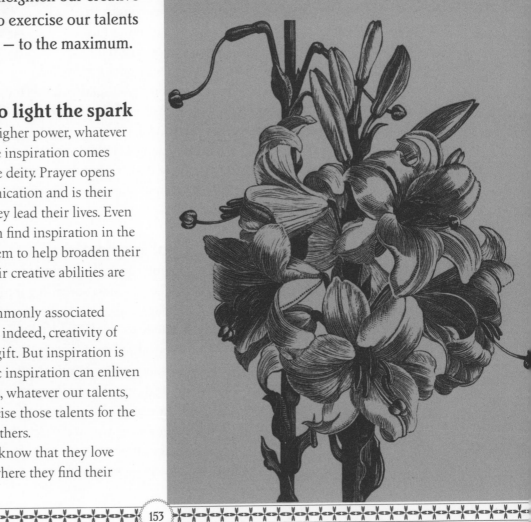

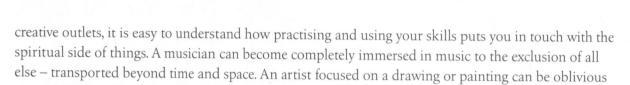

creative outlets, it is easy to understand how practising and using your skills puts you in touch with the spiritual side of things. A musician can become completely immersed in music to the exclusion of all else – transported beyond time and space. An artist focused on a drawing or painting can be oblivious to anything but the canvas. The spiritual inspiration is clear.

However, many people claim not to be creative and they may need to delve more deeply to discover what inspires them. Perhaps you cannot draw or play a musical instrument, but you may be inspired by great architecture, literature, dancing or superb scenery. We tend to think of inspiration on a large scale, but our inspiration can come from homely things, or minute details. You could find inspiration in maintaining a beautiful garden or a lovely home, caring for a child, or making anything from a cake to a card for a friend; perhaps discovering microscopic creatures inspires you. Somewhere there will be an area in which the inspirational spark can touch you: something that makes you special. Finding the right source of your personal inspiration can make the difference between feeling ordinary and feeling special.

Our angelic focus in this section falls on the archangel Gabriel, one of the only two angels mentioned by name in the Old Testament. The guardian of the Paradise to which we can only aspire, we can tap into his energies to help us find our inspiration, develop our talents and live the best life we can.

The light of inspiration

As the quotation at the beginning of this section suggests, it can be the smallest or most surprising things that light the spark of excitement in us, and it is often when we least expect it. Just as when we are dragged along to an event that doesn't sound appealing but then surprises us with its potential for enjoyment, we need to look all around us to find our inspiration. It may be one thing or many; you may have to look under many stones or in the smallest nooks and crannies, or it may be staring you in the face. But remember that we are looking into our innermost selves to find the primary source of our inspiration; as such, it will be sure to be hiding in plain sight.

The exercise for this is carried out on the floor, but you could just as easily set it up on a table if that is more convenient. You will need a large white cloth big enough for you to be able to sit on in just one corner, three jasmine or eucalyptus candles in closed lanterns, the Gabriel card from your deck of angel cards (see pages 156–159), a small glass bowl of water, some white or clear crystals or glass marbles if you wish, some dark food colouring and a cocktail stick or skewer.

❋ Spread the cloth on the floor and set up the lanterns on three corners of the cloth.

❋ Place the Gabriel card near the centre with the bowl of water next to it. Place the crystals in the water if you wish. Have the food colouring ready.

❋ Sit on the corner of the cloth which doesn't have a lantern, go through the relaxation process outlined on pages 58–62 and focus on the Gabriel card.

❋ Bring an image of Gabriel to your mind and ask him for inspiration. Think about what you would most like to do with your life and allow your subconscious to lead you where it will.

❋ Place a few drops of food colouring into the water, using the stick or skewer to drip in the colouring if the bowl is small. Agitate the water gently, if necessary, so that the colour swirls through the clear water without mixing with it.

❋ Watch the patterns, blocking out everything else. Look hard, trying to block out your conscious mind.

❋ Let the images you see guide you to thinking in new directions about the inspiration for your life. Keep Gabriel at the back of your mind and refer to him if you find you are not progressing.

❋ When you return to the everyday world, be aware that you are stronger and more imaginative because you have been in touch with Gabriel's energy.

❋ Jot down your thoughts and feelings, however irrelevant they may seem, and think about how they might help you follow an angelic lead to something special in your life.

A daily inspiration

We have already looked at decision-making with angel cards, but they can also be used for a daily affirmation to inspire you to think beyond the practicalities of just getting through the day. You can lay out a five-card spread as outlined on page 121, and turn over five cards to deal with a particular question, or simply choose a single card for the day, as described below.

You may like to use the set of angel cards you have purchased or made. You don't need to make a large set (some sets have forty or more cards). To begin with, you could make a twelve-card set based on the archangels in this book and use them to choose an inspirational message to focus on for the day. You will need postcards or index cards, pictures and adhesive or drawing materials. Alternatively, you could create the cards on a computer, then print them out on card.

❋ Draw or print out an image of each angel to stick on a postcard or index card, leaving space for your text. You can use any images you find appealing.

❋ Write an angel's name on each card, linking it with the representational image, if that is what you have chosen. If you are using general angelic images, match the name to the most appropriate image.

❋ Write the main virtues associated with each angel onto the cards. You can decide your own or choose from the list opposite.

❈	ANAEL	Calm, love, sensitivity, serenity
❈	CAMAEL	Courage in adversity, positive relationships, peace, stoicism
❈	CASSIEL	Comfort, compassion
❈	GABRIEL	Communication, creativity, inspiration, loving guidance, nurture, understanding
❈	METATRON	Clearing energy centres, efficiency, focus, growth, knowledge, logic, motivation, organization, study, thought
❈	MICHAEL	Adventure, leadership, power, protection, strength, unwavering faith
❈	RAPHAEL	Balance, harmony, healing, health, peace
❈	RAZIEL	Blessings manifest, intuition, perspective, psychic knowledge, spiritual growth, unconscious wisdom, understanding
❈	SACHIEL	Abundance, contentment, joy, prosperity
❈	SANDALPHON	Decision-making, faith, gentleness, purpose, receptivity, understanding
❈	URIEL	Adaptability, clear-sightedness, flexibility, instinctive nature, open-mindedness
❈	ZADKIEL	Appreciation, blessings, generosity

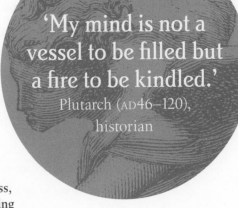

'My mind is not a vessel to be filled but a fire to be kindled.'
Plutarch (AD46–120), historian

Finish each card with an inspirational quotation or message. You could use the quotations in this book or research your own. Alternatively, you may prefer a simple message to yourself to focus on for the day.

Here are some examples of messages.

Today, I will ...

❋   ... not worry about things I cannot change.

❋   ... reach out to someone who needs help.

❋   ... be honest about my mistakes.

❋   ... take on something new.

❋   ... focus on what is most important, not irrelevant details.

❋   ... smile at everyone I see.

❋   ... spend time with someone I care for.

❋   ... see the glass half full – at least.

❋   ... learn to say 'no'.

❋   ... forgive myself for my mistakes.

❋   ... do something completely different.

❋   ... tackle a job I have been putting off.

❋   ... be proud of my achievements.

❋   ... not be afraid to ask for help.

❋   ... dismiss any feelings of guilt for things I cannot alter.

❋ ... be thankful for what I have.

❋ ... show someone how much I care.

❋ ... appreciate the good things in my life.

❋ ... spend half an hour doing nothing.

❋ ... enjoy the moment.

❋ ... change just one thing.

In the morning, set up some appropriate correspondences: silver or white crystals, such as moonstone or milky quartz and sunflowers. Burn some stimulating jasmine incense and perhaps enjoy a cup of mint tea. Sit quietly with your cards and bring the image of Gabriel into your mind. Immerse yourself in his strength. Shuffle the cards, then deal one card; or lay out all the cards face down, then use your instinct to pick one.

Think about the message on the cards and how it might apply to you today. Try to put the message into practice as you go about your day.

Bring a new world to life

Daydreaming is often considered a waste of time – an excuse for not getting on with what you are meant to be doing. Sometimes that is certainly the case. We have all probably drifted off when bored senseless by a really bad film or a dull topic of conversation at a dinner party! You recognize that feeling as you slowly drift off into another – and often far more interesting – world.

However, if you take the time to daydream in a constructive way, it can be an inspirational experience that can help in your daily life. To begin this exercise, follow your intuition. When you become practised, introduce your subconscious to an idea and allow your mind to weave the daydream around it.

You will need some myrrh or lily of the valley candles or incense, and perhaps some quiet, soothing music.

Once you are directing your daydream, it may help to have a symbol of the core idea, something as simple as a pen or a computer mouse, a rose or a key. Think about where you could most use some inspiration – a new input from deep in your instincts. If you have a new project, then that's a good place to start. Perhaps you want to think about a change you want to make to your working conditions or to your attitude towards others.

Establish your comfortable surroundings and create an atmosphere that is conducive to the thought processes. Light your candle or play some music.

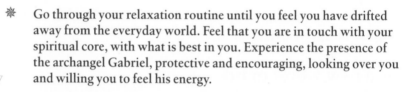

❋ Go through your relaxation routine until you feel you have drifted away from the everyday world. Feel that you are in touch with your spiritual core, with what is best in you. Experience the presence of the archangel Gabriel, protective and encouraging, looking over you and willing you to feel his energy.

❋ To begin with, simply allow your unconscious mind to lead you where it wants to go. Hold on to the positive energies and watch where your mind is taking you.

❋ If you are directing your daydream, focus on your symbol and let it fill your mind's eye. Let thoughts emerge and weave around it. Watch yourself going through an ideal scenario, if you wish, so that you can imagine how a newly inspired version of you would take things forward. Or let your imagination run riot and follow an internal logic, like Alice finding her way through Wonderland.

❋ Follow your story to a conclusion, then return to your home circumstances. What have you learnt from your freewheeling trip? Some of the ideas could well be transferred to real life and offer inspiration for your activities, while the energy of Gabriel infuses your subconscious.

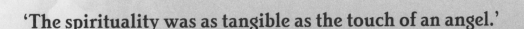

'The spirituality was as tangible as the touch of an angel.'

'I had wanted to visit Peru since I was eighteen and now, almost forty years later, we were approaching the highlight of a trip of a lifetime and had finally arrived at the hidden city of Machu Picchu. The entrance was unprepossessing – concrete, utilitarian, busy and faintly chaotic – and although neither of us admitted it at the time, we felt somewhat deflated. However, our guide's greeting was warm and enthusiastic and we followed her eagerly through the turnstile and up a steep path hemmed in on all sides by lush vegetation. Just as we were engrossed in her descriptions of her Quechua culture, she led us between two stone houses and suddenly there was this fabulous sight spread out in front of us: the temples and houses, the terraces and squares, with those iconic mountains cradling the city, dusted with curling wisps of mist.

'The beauty of it took our breath away, but it wasn't the physical beauty alone that filled our eyes with tears. There was something that took it above and beyond all definition: an energy, a spirituality that was absolutely palpable. We stood for a long time unable to speak.

'Later, we compared our experiences and both of us had felt both exposed and protected at the same time – as though some higher energy was looking deep into our souls, but not judging, simply reminding us not to forget that life benefits from a spiritual dimension and we must not ignore that in our efforts to experience the physical wonders of the world.'

MARY, BERKSHIRE, UK

Angels to protect you

A sense of security is important for us to feel calm and happy, as is the safety of those who are closest to us. If you call for angelic protection, it can ease your anxieties and make you feel more positive.

Finding an angel to help you feel secure

A feeling of security is a wonderful source of peace of mind. Children and adults who feel secure can live and grow in confidence. If you feel sufficiently secure – especially as a child – you don't even think of it as an issue and questions about insecurity may come as a surprise.

It is up to parents and others, such as family, friends, nursery staff and teachers, to provide that level of security for children for their emotional and spiritual development. By willingly putting in the hard work and commitment required, parents can ensure their children have a secure home and learn to cross the road safely, get to the top of a climbing frame, use a pair of scissors and avoid touching a hot stove.

The practical care that goes into bringing up children creates an unspoken and underlying emotional security. By taking protective measures and teaching children step by step how to protect themselves, parents are demonstrating their love every day. Without even realizing it, parents are surrounding their children with a protective sphere of love, while children subconsciously know that they are safe and secure. They do not question their inner angel because there is no possibility that he or she is wrong – children have not lost the link with their instinctive spirituality that many of us are at pains to rediscover.

Of course, life cannot be enjoyed without some risks – from

'Don't ever take the fence down until you know the reason it was put up.'
G.K. Chesterton
(1874–1936), author

childhood onwards. But it is important to minimize the more dangerous risks over which we have control – for ourselves and our children. And it is crucially important that we teach children how to look out for themselves. A child who has never handled a pair of scissors can hardly be expected to know how to use them. If a child hasn't been taught how to cross the road, he or she will be at risk when encountering busy traffic for the first time.

In addition, there are times when we all feel particularly vulnerable, when we are in need of special protection. Perhaps there is physical danger and we require additional energy to cope with it. Maybe we feel emotionally lost and need a strong, powerful love surrounding us to keep going.

So, whether it is ongoing or occasional, protecting others and protecting ourselves is a huge part of our lives. It is therefore appropriate that we choose one of the most powerful angels as the focus of our angelic protection: the archangel Michael. Think of St George and the dragon transmuted to a spiritual dimension and you have the image of Michael, the powerful and inspiring leader of the warrior angels, who can help you to triumph over evil, lead you back to confidence and strengthen your resolve. You can call on Michael's energy to maintain ongoing security for yourself and those around you, and to offer help and greater protection in difficult times.

A protective force field for your children

While teaching the practicalities of staying safe and secure shows wisdom, making an issue of emotional protection can demonstrate your own insecurity to a child. Instead, trying relating to the child on an instinctive level, using the strength and guidance of your own inner angel, to give them the best possible start. Of course, you have to get used to the fact that life will involve some bumps and bruises, tears and tantrums. But if children never experience the magical thrill of running as fast as they can along a beach or through a field just for fear (usually your fear) that they may fall, they will never learn to let their spirits soar. On a practical level, an overprotected child may never learn to fend for himself. On a spiritual level, if children experience the wonder of feeling at one with nature and going beyond themselves while it is still wholly intuitive, they will much more easily recognize and be able to seek out that feeling when they are older. They will be in touch with their inner angel and understand the value of its counsel.

Join with your child in this game of blowing bubbles. Later, it may be appropriate to discuss the symbolism of seeing your child in a protective bubble that keeps him or her from harm, and saying what that meant to you. You will need:

* a large bucket or bowl
* 2 x 1 m bamboo poles
* a roll of absorbent string or tape (some people use upholstery tape)
* gaffer tape
* liquid detergent
* glycerine
* water

First make your bubble blower. Tie a 50-cm-long piece of string or tape between the bamboo poles, about 5 cm from the ends. Tie another piece of string about 1 m long between the other ends of the poles. Tie a third piece of string just over 2 m long to this second piece of string, next to the poles. Secure with gaffer tape.

To make the bubble mixture, mix together the water, liquid detergent and glycerine in a ratio of 10:1: 25 in the bucket or bowl, and stir gently so the mixture is not frothy.

This is an outdoor activity. The best conditions are mild weather with high humidity. A sunny Sunday at midday is perfect for any activity to do with Michael. You may like to wear yellow or gold, or dress the children in yellow.

Take the two sticks and bring them together to close the loop, then dip the long loop at the top into the solution. Lift it out and slowly pull the sticks apart while you walk, or hold the blower up into a gentle breeze to create a huge bubble. Close the loop to let the bubble float free. You will need a little practice, but should soon be able to create giant bubbles.

Although this is a simple a game of giant bubbles, you can use it to bring an emotional focus to your thoughts about the importance of protecting your children. While the children are playing, take a step back for a moment and simply watch them.

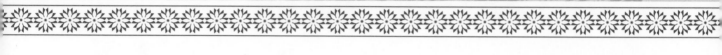

✳ Calm yourself and focus on the archangel Michael.

✳ Watch as the children create the giant bubbles and visualize them inside a vast, protective bubble created, with the help of angelic energy, by you and those near you.

✳ Really concentrate on the children's unfettered delight and how it makes you feel. Be prepared for it to be quite an emotional experience, as you share with them the joy engendered by a feeling of total security.

✳ Say a prayer, if that is appropriate for you, or silently call on Michael to remain their protector as they go about their everyday lives, and as they grow into mature and responsible adults, perhaps with children of their own. Carry Michael's protective light with you to shine on them always.

Disaster insurance

The protective energy of angels is not at your beck and call. First and foremost, you must take on the responsibility to protect yourself. On a practical level, that can mean anything from storing your kitchen

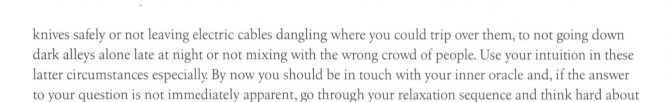

knives safely or not leaving electric cables dangling where you could trip over them, to not going down dark alleys alone late at night or not mixing with the wrong crowd of people. Use your intuition in these latter circumstances especially. By now you should be in touch with your inner oracle and, if the answer to your question is not immediately apparent, go through your relaxation sequence and think hard about the issue at hand; answers, or at least the right course to take to find them, should be available to you.

Equally, you may be one of the lucky ones who experiences a spiritual encounter when danger confronts them. One of the most common real-life angel stories reported on the internet is when someone experiences angelic help when they are in a car crash and disaster is averted in an inexplicable way. It is not possible to find an explanation. Perhaps this is a response to a silent prayer – a guardian angel finding you and saving you. Perhaps your own instincts take over to take avoidant action, a reflex so deeply buried in your subconscious that it is not perceived as your own action. Either way, the more

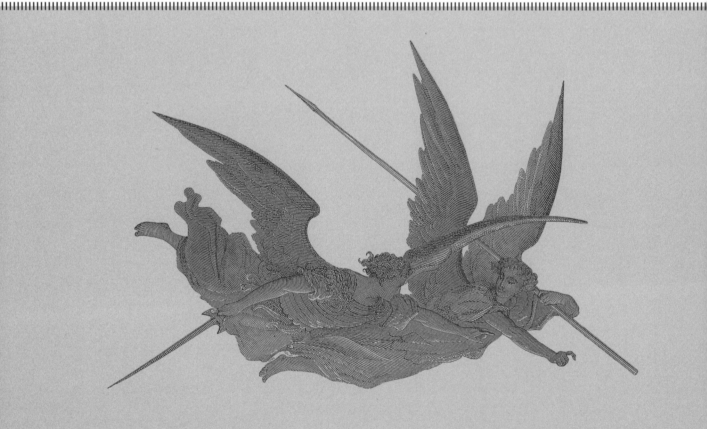

in touch you are with your inner oracle, the more likely you are to avoid such catastrophes, so – in the same way as you hope never to have to claim on an accident insurance policy – it still benefits you to try at least some of the exercises in this book and apply the principles.

A protective aura to deflect negative energies

At times we all come across people we instantly feel are emitting negative energy. The more attuned we are to the energies of our inner angel and those of other people, the more we may be affected by such outpourings of negativity. However, as kind and caring people, we do not want to shut ourselves away completely from helping people or allowing them to use us as a sounding board. For example, if your question to an old friend you have not seen for some time – a simple 'how are you?' – results in them pouring out a stream of complaints and problems, you would obviously want to help them. In doing so, however, you are at risk of absorbing so much of their negative energy that it could damage your own.

One way you can protect yourself while still offering the sympathetic ear that is clearly so desperately needed is to visualize yourself surrounded by an aura of angelic energy. You might see it as yellow or gold, offering Michael's powerful protection, or perhaps pink, bringing in the softer, conciliatory light of Anael.

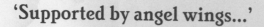

'Supported by angel wings...'

'Twelve years ago I experienced an event that I dismissed at the time, but when it happened again eight years later, I understood it was no coincidence.

'I was driving to work on a rainy day when I became distracted for a second, and when I regained my focus I realized I was too close to stationary traffic in front of me. I slammed on the brakes, fishtailed and struck the right rear of the car directly in front of me. This flipped my car into a spin, striking two more cars before it careered to the side of the road, just missing a road sign and eventually slamming into a tree. My car and the two others I had hit were destroyed. I walked out without scratch.

'During the entire episode, a warm, safe feeling enveloped me. I felt completely calm, as though someone was telling me it was okay and nothing would harm me. I vividly remember the chaos but never did I feel fear. Afterwards I assumed it was a reaction of the brain to the extreme stress of the situation and I didn't think much about it until eight years later.

'It was a rainy winter day but I needed to do an urgent repair to the roof. Even though I was worried I might slip and fall, the repair simply couldn't wait. But I needn't have worried that I would fall once I was on the roof. I put my ladder against the side of the house and, as I stepped on the top rung, the ladder slid out from beneath me.

'As I fell to the ground, the same warm feeling came over me again. This time I felt what was like two hands grabbing my shoulders. I landed straight on my feet, perfectly, as if I had been gently lowered down. The only injury was a cut on my hand from the guttering.

'I no longer think the warm feeling and safe outcome were coincidences or reactions to stressful situations. I thank the angel who protected me every day I'm alive and try to make the world a better place with my actions.'

GEORGE, SHAMONG, USA

Angels to help you cope

We all experience times when troubles press in on us, when we need to find inner reserves of strength to help us through, and the courage to keep moving forward. Look to the angel of courage in adversity.

'If you're going through hell, keep going.'
Winston Churchill (1874–1965), statesman

Finding an angel to see you through

When times are difficult, it is particularly important to have the support of others. Whether you are struggling with divorce, the loss of your job, health issues, financial troubles or relationship problems, coping alone is the most difficult thing of all. Having a loving family or loyal friends is a huge comfort in such times, and it is important to accept offers of support and help that are sincerely meant. But, equally, spiritual support is restorative to the soul and can help you turn the corner.

In the first place, contemplating your inner angel can rid you of any misplaced guilt you are harbouring about your situation. It can bring you a clearer appreciation of how you reached this point in your life, but only if you need this in order to break free of blame and recrimination.

Clarity of mind will also help you put together a plan to move slowly but surely to a better place. The deeper you are embroiled in difficulty, the harder it may be, but the light at the end of the tunnel will be your angel guiding the way.

Coping with hardship might seem endless and it requires strength and the courage to face adversity. If your courage has been tested to the limit, your angel can help you find more.

The angel to focus on to help you cope is the archangel Camael, the angel of courage in adversity. He knows we sometimes have to take on more than we think we can handle, however strong we are.

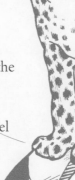

Find strength and courage

When people ask you how you cope with the problems you are experiencing, it is often difficult to know how to answer. Sometimes we have no choice but to keep drawing on our inner reserves of strength. But we can replenish those reserves by calling on the archangel Camael and asking him to share some of his strength to see us through.

If things are getting on top of you, swift action is needed – something that will give you a rush of adrenalin to kick-start your inner strength. Think of this ritual as the jump leads to a battery that reignites your spiritual motor. It might feel like the reverse of prayer or meditation, because you are using physical energy to draw in psychic energy.

Camael is often depicted as a leopard sitting on a rock. These are both symbols of the strength and stability that are the focus of this ritual.

Some people may have the strength to start this process with some physical activity – a run, a brisk walk, a swim – to activate their physical responses. If this is too much for you, simply omit this step.

* Curl up in a ball and tighten every muscle. Breathe deeply and hold all your muscles in tension for 30 seconds.

* Stretch and roar like a leopard, letting go of all your pent-up worries and frustrations.

* Feel the tension draining away and imagine you are that leopard on a rock. Feel the solid warmth beneath you, supportive and unyielding. Really experience the muscular body, the strong jaws, the feline grace.

* Lock that feeling in your image of the leopard and capture it in your inner angel so you can call on it to support you through the days ahead.

* Stay with that feeling as long as you like, then bring yourself back to the present, carrying Camael's energy with you in your innermost core.

* Make yourself an image or symbol of the leopard on a rock – a picture on the fridge door or in your pocket, for example – to remind yourself that you have inner reserves of strength and courage that will get you through.

* Then look at your most pressing problem and think of someone or something to help solve or endure it until a solution can be found.

'I know God will not give me anything I can't handle. I just wish that He didn't trust me so much.'
Mother Teresa (1910–1997), missionary

'Better by far you should forget and smile than you should remember and be sad.'
Christina Rossetti (1830–1894), poet

Learn to forgive

Guilt and responsibility are closely related; but while we need to take responsibility for our actions, guilt is a negative emotion that drains the strength we need so desperately when we are low. We need to learn to forgive ourselves for mistakes we have made and for not having all the answers, and to forgive others for what we perceive to be their failings. Because he is associated with justice and fairness, Camael can help with this. If we can love ourselves, even with all our faults, then we are less likely to blame or criticize ourselves and others.

For this exercise, you need a small tear-off pad, a black or blue pen, a red pen and a clear crystal, for balance, or a red crystal, for strength.

✳ Write in black or blue pen, on individual sheets of the pad, all the things you feel you have done that have contributed to your problem, then stack them in a pile.

✳ Write down all the things you have done to alleviate the problem or to help solve it. Put them in another pile.

✳ Count them. You may already begin to see that there are more positives than negatives.

✳ Now try your relaxation technique (see pages 58–62) for a few moments so that you feel calm and, if you can, visualize the archangel Camael. It may help to hold the crystal in your hand.

✳ Pick up each negative note and visualize yourself as Camael, offering forgiveness and understanding for your mistakes, or confirming that your choices were limited or non-existent and that you did your best. Don't make excuses, but understand and put any guilt behind you. Tick each one off in red pen, if you like. You should begin to feel the positive energy balance being restored.

✳ Carry on through the positive notes. Let your intuition guide you to an honest assessment rather than too much self-congratulation.

✳ When you have finished, visualize the angel's energy travelling into the crystal so that you can carry it with you in future and hold the angelic energy in your hand.

✳ You may need to repeat the process until you have forgiven yourself for the past and this will strengthen you for the future.

✳ Remind yourself regularly that hanging on to guilt will hold you back. Do you need to make an apology to someone to clear your conscience? If so, do it without delay and feel Camael lift a weight from your shoulders.

Bring clarity of mind

This is a simple prayer to remind us that, even in the most difficult of circumstances, there is contentment to be found in the smallest things and it is possible to find a way forward.

You will need a fragrant candle or some incense of neroli or tangerine, and a red crystal.

✳ In your safe place, light the candle or incense, hold the crystal, relax and clear your mind, then see yourself surrounded by a warm, comforting red light. Feel it like a soothing touch on your skin. Give in to the supportive embrace.

✳ Now, very slowly, watch the colour fading through the yellow of clear thought to the white of purity and balance.

✳ Look to the future with more confidence as you bring yourself back to the present, storing the positive energy to support you.

✳ It may help you to have a plan for your next actions, or it may better suit your circumstances to allow yourself to be carried forward by events. Look at your issues clearly and search your instincts to find the answers you seek.

One step at a time is enough

We may pride ourselves on our ability to multitask at times of difficulty or trauma, but we should recognize that we simply cannot do everything at once. If we try to, it will become overwhelming. It is far better to recognize our temporary limitations. Some things simply have to wait while we deal with those things we have designated as the most important. Take one step at a time and ask your angels to help you through.

'The touch was as real as anything...'

'Some years ago, I went through a life-shattering divorce soon after the birth of my son. I lived in Atlanta at the time but had to move in with my family in Chicago. It was a very dark time. I had loaded my things on a removal truck and my friend dropped us at the airport where we said goodbye. I was leaving so much behind: my marriage, my friends, my home, my job. I felt so alone with my five-month-old baby as my friend pulled away. I put Aton in his stroller and began walking to my terminal. As I was walking, I felt two firm taps on my shoulder. I turned around quickly only to find no one was there. No one was even near me! At that very second I heard the words, "You are not alone." These words were not truly audible but came as a loud inner voice, yet it was not my own "thinking voice". The taps were not a muscle twitch and were as real as anything, though they were so firm they were just shy of being uncomfortable. A feeling of love swept over me. I smiled, reassured and went home feeling much lighter. I have never felt alone again as I had done before that experience.'

ADAYA, CHICAGO, USA

Angels to bring you comfort

We often need comfort in our lives. At times of extreme stress, such as the loss of someone precious, life is hard and we value support throughout the painful process of grieving.

Finding an angel to soften sadness

Sometimes we are sad for good reason and at other times we simply feel low and need some external energy to get us going again. Perhaps we are ill and need a little looking after, or things are going badly at work, or a relationship is proving problematic. Any number of circumstances can make us unhappy.

In more extreme cases, we may have serious problems. Perhaps a change in circumstances has left

us alone, or divorce or family problems are affecting us, or, sadly, someone close to us has gone from our lives. While the settings are different and may vary in extreme, the process we go through to deal with our problem or loss is similar whether we have lost a loved one or have moved on from a long-term relationship, for example. This grieving is a process we all have to go through at some time and it is difficult. However, it is important because it teaches us to accept that the circle of life has to include bodily death. The loss we feel is painful but if we work through it, we can reach a point at which the memories, while poignant, become positive once more.

The archangel Cassiel is known as the angel of compassion, who weeps silently for our grief but can also help dry our tears. Grief of any kind puts our lives out of kilter and Cassiel can help us find the patience and strength to restore the natural balance by understanding that there are things we cannot change and that, when things move on, we can still value what has gone before.

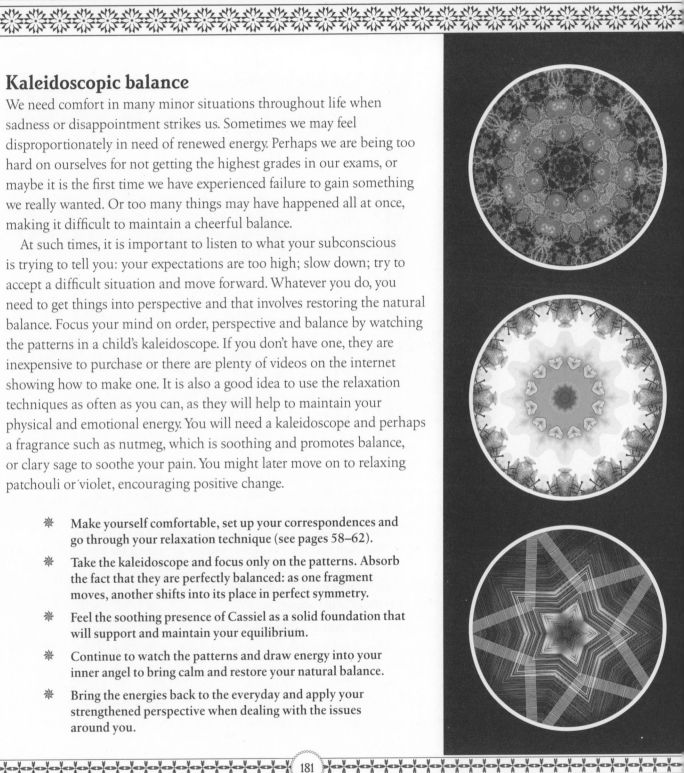

Kaleidoscopic balance

We need comfort in many minor situations throughout life when sadness or disappointment strikes us. Sometimes we may feel disproportionately in need of renewed energy. Perhaps we are being too hard on ourselves for not getting the highest grades in our exams, or maybe it is the first time we have experienced failure to gain something we really wanted. Or too many things may have happened all at once, making it difficult to maintain a cheerful balance.

At such times, it is important to listen to what your subconscious is trying to tell you: your expectations are too high; slow down; try to accept a difficult situation and move forward. Whatever you do, you need to get things into perspective and that involves restoring the natural balance. Focus your mind on order, perspective and balance by watching the patterns in a child's kaleidoscope. If you don't have one, they are inexpensive to purchase or there are plenty of videos on the internet showing how to make one. It is also a good idea to use the relaxation techniques as often as you can, as they will help to maintain your physical and emotional energy. You will need a kaleidoscope and perhaps a fragrance such as nutmeg, which is soothing and promotes balance, or clary sage to soothe your pain. You might later move on to relaxing patchouli or violet, encouraging positive change.

⁕ Make yourself comfortable, set up your correspondences and go through your relaxation technique (see pages 58–62).

⁕ Take the kaleidoscope and focus only on the patterns. Absorb the fact that they are perfectly balanced: as one fragment moves, another shifts into its place in perfect symmetry.

⁕ Feel the soothing presence of Cassiel as a solid foundation that will support and maintain your equilibrium.

⁕ Continue to watch the patterns and draw energy into your inner angel to bring calm and restore your natural balance.

⁕ Bring the energies back to the everyday and apply your strengthened perspective when dealing with the issues around you.

The grieving process

Sometimes, the comfort we need is of a more intense kind. For those left behind, the death of a loved one can be life-shattering. Even if the deceased is perhaps elderly or has been seriously ill, it is always a shock when they die and it is important that we do not ignore the impact on our lives. Because our lives have been abruptly thrown out of balance, it is likely that a rush of often conflicting emotions will struggle for control, leaving us feeling powerless and at their mercy. If we acknowledge their power and let the rollercoaster run its course, they may be less destructive. There is no point in trying to stop an incoming tide – but we can wait patiently until it turns.

As well as the greatest sadness, it is quite natural to feel other emotions, such as anger, guilt or resentment. If we acknowledge that these emotions are a result of the intensity of our feelings, then it helps us not to dwell on them.

The progress of grief is usually defined in five stages.

❋ DENIAL We all know that death will come but it is always a shock when it does. For a short time, the shock of the event can make us refuse to acknowledge that this is actually happening. Once we accept that it is, the initial response is often to think about the responsibilities of those left behind.

❋ ANGER Resentment and blame often fuel anger about the fact the event has occurred. Other negative emotions, such as guilt that you have done nothing to prevent the loss, are also common.

❋ BARGAINING This stage involves the hope that the individual can somehow postpone or delay death by some kind of bargain.

❋ DEPRESSION Life becomes colourless and without purpose.

❋ ACCEPTANCE Finally, an acknowledgement of the inevitable leads the individual to come to terms with mortality.

It is important to remember that strong emotion is physically draining. We need to allow ourselves some leeway and should try to get enough rest and sustenance. We should also try to avoid feeling

impatient that we are taking too long to heal. While we can try to help the rebalancing process, it will take its own time.

Serious trauma is a kind of grief and involves a similar process. Do not underestimate the upset and emotional pain that come with the ending of a marriage or long-term relationship, for example. You can apply the grieving support to traumatic situations, adapting it as necessary.

Flying above your troubles

When trauma occurs, it is natural to wish it would just go away. If it did, everything would be all right again, wouldn't it? Unfortunately this is impossible, but we can make an effort to rise above the difficulties that beset us, even if only temporarily, with the help of our inner angel. Visualization can help, and since Cassiel is sometimes depicted riding a dragon, he is the ideal image for lifting you out of your difficulties for a short time to give yourself some respite. You will need an indigo or black grounding crystal. You may prefer to soften it with Earth colours and energies – browns, russet, ochre – to link with Cassiel's element and to the life cycle. A soothing but refreshing fragrance, such as bergamot, would be suitable.

❊ Set up a comfortable room and use the relaxation process (see pages 58–62) you have learned to completely relax your body and mind.

❊ Visualize yourself surrounded by your problems or issues, giving them a physical form, like a crowd of people or animals.

❊ Now bring an image of Cassiel into your mind. Picture him flying above you on his dragon and actually see, in your mind's eye, his strength and confidence.

❊ Watch him fly down to land beside you, clearing a path to reach you. Look into his eyes and feel his understanding.

❊ Climb onto the dragon with him and feel yourself lifted above all your problems, focusing on his soothing energies and feeling his protection.

❊ Focus on bringing into your core the energies from outside so that you strengthen your inner angel.

Repeat a positive affirmation. A few possibilities might be:

- ❋ acceptance will help to restore the balance in my life.
- ❋ I will celebrate the life of ....
- ❋ my memories of ... will never fade.
- ❋ I know I am strong enough to get through this sad time.
- ❋ If you are grieving, visualize happy memories of your loved one and remind yourself that they will not be forgotten.
- ❋ If your problem is of another kind, visualize things going the way you would wish.
- ❋ Enjoy the experience of release, then gradually come back safely to Earth, but retain that feeling and the energy it brings to your inner angel.

Celebrating a life

You may have heard friends saying they have been to a wonderful funeral – you may have thought the same yourself and felt slightly guilty about it, but there is no reason to feel that way. A funeral is the point at which you say farewell to your loved one – leaving them in God's hands, or completing their cycle of life – and move on with your life, however slowly and gently that may need to be.

When the family and friends who attend a funeral join together to celebrate the life of the loved one, it creates a collective spirit of love and thankfulness, bringing everyone's innermost feelings together in mutual support so that each individual can find comfort in another.

If you are organizing an event in memory of a loved one, you will want to express all their best and most memorable qualities. The best way to find out what to include is to talk to other people; this will remind you of aspects of their character or events you may have forgotten about. There are many elements to think about:

- ❋ The most memorable events in their life
- ❋ Apparently insignificant events that displayed them at their best
- ❋ Their favourite books, films, TV shows, art, music
- ❋ What made them laugh

❋ Their job and career

❋ Hobbies and interests

There will be much that you will have to leave out, but a careful selection can encapsulate their life in a celebration that will help you reach the point of acceptance that is healing. After the more formal aspects of the leave-taking, try to create an opportunity for people to get together to talk about their feelings and share reminiscences. Have some photograph albums if you can. Don't be surprised if, after a short while, there is laughter mixed with the sadness; this is a good sign that you are remembering fondly but are also able to let go.

A memory box

Some counsellors suggest to children that they should make a memory box for, say, a grandparent who has died. This idea should not necessarily be confined to children. Seeking emotional healing could help comfort you by seeing the cycle of the deceased's life in the bigger context.

You might include photographs, mementos, perhaps some pressed flowers or things that remind you of the person. If your grandfather liked a particular comedian, include a picture of him or a note of some of his jokes. A family tree is an interesting inclusion, as it so clearly demonstrates the natural movement of time through the generations. When you take out your box, remember to relax first and bring to mind all the good memories so that they strengthen and soothe your inner angel.

'An angel told me I was not alone...'

'I was riding my bike down the road near my home; it was the weekend but there wasn't much traffic about. Suddenly a car came out from a side road without looking, right into my path. I swerved to try to avoid him but there was no way I could have got out of his way in time. He hit me side on and I was somersaulted up in the air and smashed down on to the bonnet of his car.

'Miraculously, I rolled off the bonnet and mentally checked myself over – not a scratch. I picked up my bike – perhaps that paint chip wasn't there before, but it was otherwise perfect. The guy's bonnet was another story – it was dented in and scratched, a real mess. Fortunately, the driver was also unhurt, but he and the onlookers were equally surprised that I had come out of it unscathed. One said, "I had my hand on my phone ready to call the ambulance. I couldn't believe it when you stood up!"

'I got back on my bike to ride home and put my earphones on. Immediately I heard one of my favourite songs, "You Are Not Alone". I've always found it comforting but this time I really felt that it was giving me a specific message and that someone, or some energy, had been watching over me that day. That's a very special feeling and I experience it again every time I hear that song.'

ADRIAN, BERKSHIRE, UK

Angels to bring you contentment

'Contentment is natural wealth, luxury is artificial poverty.'
Socrates (470–399BC), philosopher

The smell of freshly baked bread, the laughter of a child – how often do we rush about our daily lives and brush past the joy these simple things can give us? Let angels help you see the wonder in simplicity.

Finding an angel to share your joy

Sometimes life just gets too complicated and we move along so fast that we don't appreciate what we have or really enjoy what we are doing. If we are always focused on what is next, we cannot fully enjoy what we are doing now, so we need to teach ourselves to slow down – stop, even – and appreciate the tiny details that can bring intense joy and offer a wonderful source of new energy.

Do you remember stopping to watch the little bird in the garden for a few precious moments? That is the feeling to search for because it is wonderfully uplifting when you begin to experience beauty at that level. It feeds into your inner angel, filling your energy stores with positivity. And it is something you can do every day; it is not confined to rare special occasions.

To illustrate the quotation above, you can contrast two possibilities on an everyday level to show that the greatest luxuries are not necessarily the things that give the most pleasure or, more importantly, bring the greatest joy. To be wined and dined among strangers in a five-star restaurant would certainly be a

treat but, if it happens at all, it might only be once or twice in a lifetime. If you only had to feed your energies on such occasions, most of us would be spiritually hungry much of the time. But you will often have the chance to share a modest meal with family and friends. So what if it's fish and chips, not Beluga caviar? You can appreciate it and soak up the positive energy of the occasion with just as much ease if you focus on really appreciating what you have.

Sachiel is our chosen angel here, as he is a benefactor bringing abundance and encourages us to appreciate and enjoy, bringing us towards being content with what we have because we extract every tiny bit of goodness from everything we touch and experience.

Sensory contentment

In this exercise, the idea is to bring to mind as many things as you can that bring you joy, working one at a time on each of your senses. Don't tackle all your senses at once, but take your time and do the exercise separately for each one.

You will need crystals in blue or purple: amethyst, lapis lazuli, sapphire, sugalite or topaz might be appropriate to set the scene. You could use incense or candles of lemon balm or pennyroyal, which are harmonizing and energizing.

- ❋ Start by creating the atmosphere, as usual, with comfort and relaxation in mind.
- ❋ Relax and take your mind away until you can visualize Sachiel, surrounded by a blue aura, perhaps holding a sheaf of corn.
- ❋ Think about the things that have brought your inner angel the greatest pleasure or inspiration – the greatest lift to your spirit. These may include the context in which you enjoyed them. They may be major things or small things. For example, you could include seeing the pyramids at Giza in the company of someone you love, or seeing an unusual bird in the hedgerow for the very first time. It could be the taste of an exquisite dessert at a top celebrity-chef restaurant, or the last time you shared a chicken sandwich with your mum.

✳ In each case, use your visualization techniques to let your inner angel experience these joys once again. (It seems there are no equivalent words for the other senses!)

✳ Concentrate on your sense of sight. What are the most beautiful sights you have seen? It could be anything from Machu Picchu in Peru or the Statue of Liberty in New York to a stunning flower or a pressed and faded bud from your wedding bouquet.

✳ Concentrate on your sense of hearing. Which sounds have brought you the greatest joy? Could it be your favourite CD, a fabulous concert, or your child singing in the primary school choir?

✳ Concentrate on your sense of taste. Define your favourite foods and when you enjoyed them. Was it a costly meal at a fabulous restaurant, or the cake your niece baked for your birthday?

✳ Concentrate on your sense of smell. This is most likely to be hugely evocative: the salt smell of the sea on a warm breeze, a beautiful rose fragrance, the smell of the freshly baked bread your mother used to make on a Sunday.

✳ Concentrate on your sense of touch. The feel of silk or satin on your skin might be your choice, or perhaps the joy you experienced when stroking a favourite pet, or the touch of a lover.

✳ Finally, concentrate on your sixth sense – anything you cannot specifically attribute to the five other senses. It could anything from holding your baby for the first time to the feeling you experience when standing on a windy hillside.

✳ When you bring yourself back to reality, store the energy of these experiences in your image of Cassiel to remind you to keep looking for contentment every day.

Microscopic contentment

You can do a similar exercise, looking for any kind of experience that made you feel 'wow, that's amazing', starting with large things, then going down in size until you can identify the smallest thing you can think of that brought that energy rush. It is an exercise you can repeat as often as you like, starting again each time where you left off in your ever-decreasing scale. You can include anything in your list at all – from physical things to experiences or events. It will be impossible to define many things strictly by size, of course, but place it where it feels right. You might start with the Taj Mahal, the Grand Palace in Bangkok, the Natural History Museum in London or the Great Wall of China, then work down through your favourite painting or piece of music to the smell of flowers and a drop of dew on the morning grass. Perhaps you can then employ a magnifying glass – readily available in children's stores, sewing shops or stamp collectors' shops – or even a microscope, if you have access to one.

Each time you come back to the real world, remember to store the energy you have gained from the visualization so you can bring that energy to bear when you think of your image of Cassiel.

'Her favourite painting was *The Great Piece of Turf...*'

'Some people believe that we become angels – or something like angels – when we die but I don't subscribe to that. But I do believe that, in this life, we can reach for something more than the ordinary and everyday, something that pulls at our emotions or lifts us beyond everything.

'A former colleague of mine, who sadly passed away a short while ago, is my constant reminder of that. She was a humanist so did not believe in God or a life after death, but that didn't mean she didn't believe in spiritual things. And one of the things I remember most about her was the excitement she felt when she heard that her favourite painting, *The Great Piece of Turf* by Albrecht Dürer, was coming to London and she could actually see the original.

'It's just a small painting, only 41cm x 32cm, showing, not surprisingly, a tiny area of mixed grasses, but she could stare at it for hours, taken completely out of this world, with this look of joy on her face. Nothing mattered then. She found such a spiritual lift from that tiny canvas that I think she was as near communing with the angels then as anyone will ever be.'

SUE, SLOUGH, UK

Angels to celebrate with you

Celebrations mark milestones in our lives: the birth of a child, a wedding, a christening, an anniversary. Bringing a spiritual dimension to your joy can only lift your spirits higher.

Finding an angel to join the party

It is no surprise that the greatest lifts to our inner angel result from the joyous times in our lives when we celebrate special occasions. What else would such events do for our spirits than bring them a rush of positive energy? These incidents can range from the smallest celebration – for getting to the end of a difficult week or finishing a project you have been working on – to one of life's major events – a special birthday, a family wedding or the birth of a child.

Do you need to think about angels at this time? Some would say not, but being in touch with your inner angel is an ongoing commitment, through the good times and the bad, and if you are really in tune with your intuitive self, you can imbue yourself with the energy of such as occasion to take forward into the rest of your life. Getting in touch with the angels can intensify these wonderful experiences and bring them to a spiritual level. Besides, perhaps you have an excess of energy to spare.

The archangel Zadkiel is the soul of generosity, filled with benevolence, concerned with ensuring balance and harmony and making sure there is a just distribution of resources. Zadkiel will bring joy to the celebration of harmonious times.

Party prayer

You can use Zadkiel's energy to give thanks for the joy of any celebration in your life. Ask the key players to arrive early at the event and to bring a small gift of some kind to celebrate the occasion. This could be an item of food or drink, flowers or a token gift. You will need your chosen correspondences, your friends and a token gift each. Try a blue candle, perhaps with some sprigs of fresh, enlivening rosemary or refreshing sage to fragrance the room.

❋ Arrange the space so that you have room to sit or stand in a circle, inside or outside, as you prefer. Light the candle in the centre and sit round the table.

❋ Ask each person to place their gift on the table.

❋ Hold hands and say a few words of thanks to Zadkiel for the joy the occasion will bring.

❋ Each individual may like to say what the occasion means to him or her.

❋ Take some photographs to remind you of the occasion and think about Zadkiel's energy when you look back and enjoy them.

Childlike enjoyment

We have already touched on the fact that children think intuitively rather than rationally. The distinction between fantasy and reality that is so important for adults is often irrelevant for children. While playing an imaginative game, for example, a child's doll can actually walk and talk, or a teddy bear can fly a plane. The child will hold a perfectly natural-sounding conversation with thin air as if, in his or her mind, a friend – or an angel – is standing there.

When we are happy, it is much easier to get back to this kind of innocent enjoyment, to let go and feel absolutely free of the constraints of logic. When you play with your children or grandchildren, immerse yourself in the experience and allow yourself to believe with them. Follow your instincts and indulge your intuitive self. This will exercise your sense of what is good and natural, so that when you work on angelic contact you will be more able to activate your inner oracle. It will help you to relax into your angelic experiences and trust yourself to find out what is best.

> 'Celebrate what you want to see more of.'
> Tom Peters (b. 1942), businessman

If you find it hard to do this, dig out some old photographs of yourself as a child and try the following exercise:

* Look through the photos with a friend or member of your family and talk about what you see in those pictures.

* Alternatively, you might prefer to do this on your own, in which case it is likely to be more contemplative.

* If you have a few pictures of a particularly memorable occasion, narrow your search to those images. You are more likely to remember details of such an event.

* Start with the broader physical details: where you were, the circumstances in which the photograph was taken, the date, who took the photograph. Paint the background to the picture in your mind and try to experience it as best you can.

* Move on to the detail. Who you were with? What you were you wearing? What was your hairstyle like? Can you remember what those clothes felt like? Was the fabric rough or soft? Did you like or hate the new shoes?

* Begin to move inside your child self. What did it feel like? Can you get right inside that child and feel the excitement at the birthday party, remember the sea breeze on your face on that beach holiday? Travel back in your mind to that innocent and instinctive enjoyment.

Try to remember that feeling when you celebrate the joyous times in your life. You can carry its purity with you throughout your adulthood to help you keep in touch with the inner angel who can guide you on your way.

'Angels help me celebrate my life...'

'Summer brings with it the fun of many celebrations, from cookouts to pool parties. But you don't have to wait for an invitation to a special event to celebrate.

'Angels remind us that we have something to celebrate all the time: God's love. The world's major religions say that angels celebrate God's love in heaven constantly by singing. Surely they celebrate the good news that they're able to deliver to people as well.

'In heaven, angels do much more than just sitting around on clouds like they do in cartoons. They're actively engaged in joyful work. Angels are partying in heaven right now! They could even be eating cake as they celebrate.

'Since you're not living in heaven yet, your circumstances may change from good to bad and back again. But God doesn't change, and I believe that nothing can change his love for you and me. So, just like the angels, you've got something to celebrate – even if your summer isn't starting off very well.

'When you make the choice to celebrate what you can right now, you'll start to notice more reasons to celebrate. And if you make celebrating a habit, you'll be in good company, because that's what angels do.'

WHITNEY HOPLER, ANGELS AND MIRACLES (HTTP://ANGELS.ABOUT.COM)

Your guardian angel

If you have worked hard in your search for your inner angel, then hopefully you will have been successful in getting in touch with your spiritual core — your inner angel oracle — to help and guide you through life.

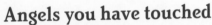

Angels you have touched

Throughout this book you have been encouraged to access the supportive energies of your angel oracle. Hopefully you have succeeded and found that by staying in constant touch with what is fundamentally good and honest in your soul, your decision-making is more straightforward, your choices more often beneficial and your satisfaction with the path of your life improved. You have learned relaxation techniques to soothe stress, visualization to enhance your energy levels and determination, and discovered various ways of getting to the heart of what you want out of life and what you can put back into it.

For some, this will have been a personal journey through their subconscious to the source of their spiritual goodness,. They will have found restorative energy from their own inner reserves, from those close to them — the 'earth angels' all around us — and from the effervescent spring of energy that is created by the wonder of life itself.

Others will have found that this inner angel is their way of contacting a higher, more spiritual plane where divine messengers wait to support, guide and protect us. This experience may have strengthened their faith in a divine being. Whether a personal journey or the confirmation of a divine presence, both experiences are equally valid.

Look inside for your guardian angel

A guardian angel is a divine being who walks with you through your life to guide and protect you. It is a being uniquely assigned to you

> 'Life begets life. Energy creates energy. It is by spending oneself that one becomes rich.'
> Sarah Bernhardt (1844–1923), actor

who is always there as a sounding board for problems, to bring you comfort and encouragement, to protect you from harm and bring you peace.

If you belong to the first group of people, believing in the strength of the inner spirit, the idea of a guardian angel may be hard to believe. For these people, the guardian angel can perhaps be identified as an individual's spiritual conscience. This can feel just as real as an external being. You might like to give your guardian angel a name and think about his character traits – the parts of you that are good, spiritual and admirable. When you have an important decision to make, discuss it with your guardian angel; in order to test the arguments, let him put one point of view while you take the opposite side. Meditate on your guardian angel when your energies are low, or you are feeling down and in need of comfort so that you can restore your natural energies. If you are in a strange place, feeling threatened or out of your comfort zone in any way, imagine your guardian angel walking next to you and be encouraged by his protective guidance.

Remember, too, that your guardian angel can grow with you. As you learn more about yourself and your subconscious, as you grow in understanding as a person, your inner guardian angel will mature and grow with you, and always be there to lead you along the right path.

Look above for your guardian angel

Those with faith in the divine are likely to understand the concept of a guardian angel in a different way. Irish mystic Lorna Byrne explains how she sees angels every day, observing that each one of us has his or her own guardian angel standing behind us. She smiles when people deny the existence of a guardian angel because, at that precise moment, she can see the angel right behind them. There are many others who have seen, or experienced, the help of their guardian angel, often in dramatic circumstances when they have been rescued from a dangerous situation, but sometimes simply as a quiet presence, always there to support and protect them and to bring them closer to their god.

If you have identified your guardian angel, then you will know how much you rely on him to strengthen your convictions and keep you on a righteous and spiritual path. Whether you have encountered him on only one occasion or, like Lorna, he is a regular feature of your life, once you have experienced him your faith is likely to be unshakeable.

Who might your guardian angel be?

As only a small selection of angels are the focus of this book, you may not be able to identify your guardian angel among them. You might need a broader scope to find out more. The most important thing is to recognize and acknowledge your guardian angel's presence and benefit from his energy. The following suggestions might offer you further food for thought if you wish to find out more. Look on websites or in books such as *A Dictionary of Angels* by Gustav Davidson or by angel specialists such as Doreen Virtue and Diana Cooper. If you feel your guardian angel is associated with the season or the month when you first experienced his presence, this can help you in your search.

ANGELS OF THE SEASONS

As well as the archangels Raphael, Michael, Gabriel and Uriel, other angels are linked with the seasons.

❋	**Spring**	Amatiel, Caracasa, Commissoros, Core, Spugliguel
❋	**Summer**	Gargatel, Gaviel, Tariel, Tubiel.
❋	**Autumn**	Guabarel, Tarquam, Torquaret
❋	**Winter**	Amabael, Attarib, Ceterari

ANGELS OF THE MONTH AND ZODIAC

Angels are associated with each month of the year and also with the astrological signs of the zodiac.

❋	**January and Aquarius**	(21 January–19 February)	Gabriel
❋	**February and Pisces**	(20 February–20 March)	Barchiel
❋	**March and Aries**	(21 March–19 April)	Machidiel

❊	**April and Taurus**	(20 April–20 May)	Asmodel
❊	**May and Gemini**	(21 May–21 June)	Ambriel
❊	**June and Cancer**	(22 June–22 July)	Muriel
❊	**July and Leo**	(23 July–22 August)	Verchiel
❊	**August and Virgo**	(23 August–22 September)	Hamaliel
❊	**September and Libra**	(23 September–22 October)	Uriel
❊	**October and Scorpio**	(23 October–22 November)	Barbiel
❊	**November and Sagittarius**	(23 November–21 December)	Adnachiel
❊	**December and Capricorn**	(22 December–20 January)	Anael

ANGELS OF THE DAYS

Some sources suggest a specific angel supervises each day, other sources indicate that the hours of the day are governed in rotation by seven angels: Michael, Anael, Raphael, Gabriel, Cassiel, Sachiel and Camael.

❊	**Monday**	Gabriel
❊	**Tuesday**	Camael
❊	**Wednesday**	Raphael
❊	**Thursday**	Sachiel, Sandalphon
❊	**Friday**	Anael
❊	**Saturday**	Cassiel, Uriel
❊	**Sunday**	Michael, Metatron

ANGELS OF THE NATURAL WORLD

Several angels are associated with the Earth and other aspects of the cosmos.

❊	**Earth**	Azriel, Admael, Arkiel, Arciciah, Ariel, Harabael, Saragael, Yabbashael
❊	**Moon**	Kakabel
❊	**Elements**	Ariel (Earth), Cherub (Air), Seraph (Fire), Tharsis (Water)
❊	**Forests**	Zilphas
❊	**Mountains**	Rampel
❊	**Sea**	Rahab
❊	**Water**	Tharsis, Arariel, Talliud
❊	**Winds**	Uriel (South), Michael (East), Raphael (West), Gabriel (North). Interestingly, these do not relate to the directions with which they are associated.

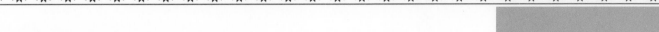

ANGELS OF PRINCIPLE AND EMOTION

Concepts and qualities we know and understand, but which do not have a physical expression, are represented by specific angels.

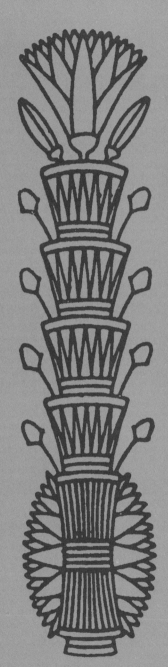

❋	**Agriculture**	Risnuch
❋	**Benevolence**	Zadkiel, Achsah, Hasdiel
❋	**Compassion**	Rachmiel, Raphael
❋	**Enlightenment**	Jophiel
❋	**Fertility**	Samandiriel
❋	**Freedom**	Nisroc
❋	**Friendship**	Mihr
❋	**Commerce**	Anauel
❋	**Heroism**	Narsinha
❋	**Hope**	Phanuel
❋	**Invention**	Liwet
❋	**Joy**	Gabriel, Raphael
❋	**Justice**	Tsadkiel, Azza
❋	**Law**	Dina
❋	**Imagination**	Samandiriel
❋	**Integrity**	Haamiah
❋	**Kindness**	Hael
❋	**Light**	Gabriel, Isaac
❋	**Love**	Hadraniel, Raphael, Theliel, Rahmiel
❋	**Patience**	Achaiah
❋	**Peace**	Gabriel
❋	**Prayer**	Akatriel, Gabriel, Metatron, Raphael, Sandalphon
❋	**Respect**	Rehael
❋	**Science**	Raphael
❋	**Silence**	Shateiel
❋	**Song**	Israfil
❋	**Success**	Perpetiel
❋	**Truth**	Amitiel, Michael, Gabriel

'I can hear the comforting voice to this day...'

'I was travelling home one evening from work; it was about 6:20 pm and had just started raining. I had just topped a hill and noticed a car coming towards me at high speed, still at a distance but getting quickly closer. I changed lanes to avoid the car hitting me, but it changed with me, heading straight at me. I changed back to the first lane but again the other car moved with me. I realized there was nothing I could do to prevent a collision so I gripped the steering wheel, hit the brakes, shut my eyes and cried out, "Dear Jesus".

'As the vehicle hit me head on at about 85 mph, I felt something holding around me, like a great big hug. Then everything went blank. When I came to, I was lying half way out of my vehicle on the other side of the highway. Someone, who could have been male or female, was sitting with me, shielding me from the rain and assuring me that help would soon come. The engine and transmission were resting on my legs inside the car and I could not move. Then I passed out again. I woke up as multiple fire fighters, medics and police officers managed to free me from the car and rush me to hospital where I found that my hips and pelvis had been crushed, and I suffered a haematoma on the left side of my brain. The young man driving the other car died immediately; his injured passenger admitted to investigators that they were playing "chicken" with other drivers. They told me that my seat belts detached when my car door was ripped open on impact, so there were no safety devices to hold me in. The doctors were amazed that I lived. More than that, I recovered from several operations and am back to 100 per cent now.

'After the crash, I wanted to thank the person who had stayed by my side until rescue arrived but the police insisted that when they arrived, there was no one else there.

'I can remember the comforting voice as if I heard it yesterday although I could not describe the look, or even if it was male or female.

'This is when I realized that I had an angel caring for me. '

RUNNING BEAR, USA

Move forward with your angel oracle

However you have experienced your angel, it will be of huge benefit because knowing yourself, deep in your subconscious, will help you find a happier and more fulfilling path through life.

Keeping in touch with your inner angel is a lifetime commitment where you continually learn more about what it is that really matters to you and how to put into practice all the finest hopes and dreams you have for your life. It places you at the heart of the decision-making process, while ensuring that your decisions are not motivated by selfish or egotistical impulses. The link with this spiritual energy shows you, above all, how interdependent we all are, and how vital it is for our well-being to learn to respect one another's opinions, intentions, strengths and weaknesses. If you have truly tuned in to your inner angel oracle you will have learned a great deal about yourself.

※ INTUITION Trust your intuition to guide you. Its source is your subconscious mind, which knows what is good and what is best for you.

※ TRUST Angel contact is based on spiritual goodness, so you can trust the messages.

※ HONESTY Be honest with yourself; only then will the outcome be beneficial.

※ RESPONSIBILITY Each of us must take responsibility for our own decisions and actions.

※ SHARING Sharing can assuage grief and increase joy.

※ SELFLESSNESS Your decisions are your responsibility but will take into account all those whose lives touch your own.

※ SUPPORT While we are there for others, we also gain from their support.

I hope you continue to talk to your angel oracle and listen to his advice, and that your joys and celebrations are the most memorable aspects of your life.

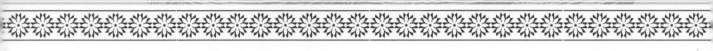

Finding help and support